T5-BBZ-435

The Organization of Schooling

The Organization of Schooling

A Study of Educational Grouping Practices

by Afred Yates
Department of Educational Studies
University of Oxford

LONDON
ROUTLEDGE & KEGAN PAUL

First published in 1971
by Routledge & Kegan Paul Ltd
Broadway House, 68-74 Carter Lane
London EC4V 5EL
Printed in Great Britain by
Northumberland Press Ltd
Gateshead 8
© Alfred Yates 1971
ISBN 0 7100 7047 0 (c)
ISBN 0 7100 7048 9 (p)

THE STUDENTS LIBRARY OF EDUCATION has been designed to meet the needs of students of Education at Colleges of Education, and at University Institutes and Departments. It will also be valuable for practising teachers and educationists. The series takes full account of the latest developments in teacher-training and of new methods and approaches in education. Separate volumes will provide authoritative and up-to-date accounts of the topics within the major fields of sociology, philosophy and history of education, educational psychology and method. Care has been taken that specialist topics are treated lucidly and usefully for the non-specialist reader. Altogether, the Students' Library of Education will provide a comprehensive introduction and guide to anyone concerned with the study of education and with educational theory and practice.

J. W. TIBBLE

So far as organizing the conditions of learning is concerned, there are few things which are known to be certainly true. One is the individual nature of all learning and hence the need for some learning process to be organized on a fairly strictly individualized basis. There are two co-relatives of this, also certainly true. Some things are better learned by some children in groups than individually, because given the appropriate conditions many (but not all) children learn some things more easily from one another rather than from adults. Secondly some other things by their very nature can only be learned in groups, e.g. how to work together to discover and attain common ends and, of course, all those activities which are by their nature group activities, like playing in an orchestra, acting in a play or working or playing in a team. But when we come to examine educational practices we find that the crucial factors in decisions about grouping are either economic or are based on opinions which have been but little influenced by research.

How should children be grouped for learning; within the education system as a whole (i.e. into schools), within schools (i.e. into 'classes' or other basic units) and within basic units, whatever these may be? These are the general issues behind our current debates, on tripartite or comprehensive, on single-sex or mixed, on streaming, tracking, setting or family grouping? These in turn are closely related to questions concerning when compulsory schooling should begin, at five, six or seven, and when it should end, at fifteen, sixteen or even eighteen, and also whether there should be well-defined breaks in the process and if so when —at eight, eleven, twelve, thirteen, fifteen and so on.

In this book Alfred Yates provides an overall perspective on the problems of how children come to be allocated to various educational groups. He shows how uncertain, in terms of educational benefit, are many of the criteria that we use for such allocation, and describes the unforeseen consequences that our decisions often entail. Without recourse to the technical language that makes research reports difficult reading for student and layman, but without underestimating the complexity of the issues involved this informed study brings together the findings of a large number of researches which bear upon these problems.

This book should be required reading, not only for students in colleges and departments of education, but for all those who are involved, whether as teachers, parents or members of local authorities, in decisions that have such a great effect on children's future.

BEN MORRIS

Contents

CONTENTS

Introduction

Before attempting to make an omelette, Mrs Beeton prudently advised, first take a dozen eggs. By the same token, any prescription for the effective organization of schooling must include, at the outset, appropriate arrangements for assembling groups of pupils.

On the face of it, this would seem to be a fairly straightforward undertaking, calling for no more than a modest degree of administrative competence. In the event it has proved to be an intractable problem for which a generally acceptable solution has still to be found.

The procedures for associating pupils and teachers are described in the technical literature on the subject as *grouping* practices or operations. These involve, in effect, progressive degrees of sampling and sub-sampling whereby an initially amorphous population is transformed into a series of fully operational educational units. The task may be said to be successfully completed when every pupil has a desk in a classroom, a place at a laboratory bench, a position in a football team, a peg in a cloakroom, or whatever else may be required to satisfy his educational needs, and when he, his parents, his teachers and all others who are entitled to be concerned, have expressed their full satisfaction with the arrangements that have been made.

The initial grouping operation that we are required to

undertake is that of assembling, notionally, those for whom education is to be provided. Of the total population at any given moment only a minority is designated for full-time schooling. The constitution of this sample depends in part on the resources that are made available for educational purposes and in part on prevailing notions concerning the length of the period of schooling that is required to satisfy individual needs and the demands of the community.

We may readily dismiss as impracticable the extreme possibilities of either housing all the members of this defined educable population within a single institution or of affording them instruction within their own homes. The need is manifest for a further process of differentiation which will yield separate groups of manageable size. In other words, if schools did not already exist, we should find it necessary to invent them.

To proceed with this second or *inter-school* grouping stage it would seem to be necessary to have some notion of how large or small a school ought to be if it is to be effectively organized. This question bears some resemblance to those that small boys delight in posing and of which a typical example is: how long is a piece of string? The acceptable answer, I seem to remember, is that it depends. Fortunately, perhaps, the durability of school buildings and their relatively inflexible proportions permit us to postpone any firm decision on this issue. The immediate practical problem with which we are confronted at this stage is that of distributing pupils among the schools that are at present available. Nevertheless we ought to be preparing ourselves to meet the possibility that at some time in the future funds may be provided for building new schools and for replacing those that have become obsolete. To this end we shall need to examine the concept of an optimal size for schools of various kinds.

Although the sizes of the school buildings available to us largely determine the number of pupils we can assign to each of them, we have a considerable range of choice when we come to consider the composition of a school's intake. If for example, we have 1,000 pupils and two schools housing 250 and 750 pupils respectively, there are, theoretically, millions of ways in which the inter-school grouping could be effected.

One simple method of achieving this, which would give absolute priority to the principle of equality of opportunity, would be to employ a process of random sampling. By definition this would accord to each pupil an equal chance of being assigned to a particular school. The first of many snags that we would encounter if we were rash enough to make this attempt is that the notional list of pupils that we compiled at the outset includes some who could not be included in the sampling process. There are some parents who prefer to make their own arrangements for the education of their children and are prepared to bear the considerable expense that this involves. Having amended the list to allow for these withdrawals, we would then encounter a further group of parents who, although willing to participate in the publicly provided system, enter certain caveats about the kind of school to which they are prepared to send their children and about the sort of education that they require for them. Those who belong to a distinctive religious sect, for example, may stipulate that their children should be associated with teachers and fellow pupils who share their faith.

If we were now to proceed with our intentions, dealing with the reduced but still sizeable group of pupils on whose behalf no protests had as yet been lodged, we should soon encounter further opposition—this time from tax-payers as well as parents. We would learn that considerations of cost and convenience, as well as apparent fairness, need to be borne in mind. Our computer, for example, may have ordained that a child in Carlisle should attend a day school in Penzance. This kind of difficulty, of course, we could readily overcome by inventing local education authorities. If assignments to schools were arranged independently within each locality, we might still be able to cling to the principle of randomness.

At this point, inevitably, we should begin to hear from a section of the community that during this imaginary saga has so far remained uncharacteristically silent. Schools, we would discover, are staffed by teachers, who have views, which they are prepared to express, on the composition of a school community. Our inept but well-intentioned attempts might, for example, have resulted in a group of infants being entrusted to the care of teachers whose special forte is the preparation of sixth formers for 'A'-level examinations. We should find ourselves being reminded forcibly that there are important educational considerations to be taken into account when allocating pupils to schools. Nor would it afford us much comfort to learn that teachers disagree violently amongst themselves as to what the nature and relevance of these educational considerations might be. Indeed this serves rather to add to the complexity of our task.

Although only a selection of the problems involved in inter-school grouping has been considered in the foregoing discussion it will come as no surprise to the reader to learn that a wide variety of procedures have been developed for this purpose, some of them calling for a considerable degree of administrative ingenuity. The characteristic that they have in common is that they all attract criticism in some measure, and, again, some of the reasons for this have been suggested. What is sometimes found more difficult to understand, particularly by those who are unfamiliar with the ways in which we order our educational affairs in this country, is why some of the controversies that surround this aspect of grouping are so intensely passionate. Most educational issues give rise to debate and disagreement and it is highly desirable that they should do so. What we elect to do with, for and, sometimes, to children in the schools ought to be matters of concern not only to their parents but to adult citizens generally. And, indeed, we can usually count on some public interest being displayed in any suggested educational innovation. Proposals to change methods of teaching or to modify the school curriculum are not only anxiously scrutinized by parents but are critically examined in newspaper articles and correspondence. The debates on matters of this kind, however, are usually conducted in a relatively low key and although rational argument may not eventually prevail over prejudice, at least the former commands a fair hearing.

The differences of view about some aspects of inter-school grouping, however, are of an altogether different character, often involving deeper emotional responses than the issues themselves would appear to warrant. There are, for example, teachers in independent schools who are on record as having threatened to emigrate or to take up market gardening if their establishments are integrated within the publicly maintained system; and some of those in grammar schools are inclined to adopt a comparable posture when the possibility of reorganization along comprehensive lines is discussed. These are not the kind of reactions that can be explained solely in terms of differences of opinion about the extent to which alternative administrative arrangements are conducive to children's educational progress. Teachers clearly perceive certain forms of grouping as potential threats to their own status and security.

Comparable attitudes may be discerned also among parents and the public at large. This is because some forms of grouping are regarded, and not without justification, as serving to support the present structure of society and others as being capable of modifying it. The British enjoy a well-deserved reputation for maintaining relatively unobtrusive class distinctions. The secret of our success rests partly on the operation of an effective system of promotion and relegation, but more particularly on our genius for so grading institutions and amenities as to minimize the risk of embarrassing encounters between members of different social strata. A man may drink, for example, in his club, in an hotel lounge or in a public house. And the latter can usually offer a choice between a saloon and a public bar.

Our educational system reflects, to some extent, the social divisions that characterize society as a whole. We have developed not only a variety of schools but a recognizable hierarchy amongst them. Furthermore these distinctions are not without significance in terms of the ways in which privileges and opportunities for advancement are distributed. It is undeniable that mere proof of attendance at one type of school may be more serviceable to an individual in certain respects than a distinguished record of effort and achievement at another.

In these circumstances, any proposal for modifying existing inter-school grouping practices may be interpreted as a subversive measure, especially if it envisages a reduction in the number of available categories or types of school and, consequently, the merging of groups that have grown accustomed to separate identities.

We must now turn to the third stage in the grouping process. One would need to get up early in the morning to discover all the members of a particular school assembled together. For the greater part of each working day they are distributed among separate classrooms, laboratories, gymnasia and playing fields in groups of varying size and composition. The term *intra-school* grouping is used to describe the operations that are involved in assigning pupils

to the separate units into which a school is normally
divided. In a large secondary school, this is a complex
undertaking involving not only progressive degrees of sub-
division but also some cross-classification. Thus, there
might be an initial division into lower, middle and upper
sections of the school, followed by further divisions into
courses, 'sides', etc., and, within these, into classes or sets.
At the same time the school might choose to operate
grouping procedures which involve associating pupils who,
for other purposes, are in separate sections. For example,
a house or tutorial group may contain members drawn from
all the smaller units into which the school is normally
divided for teaching purposes, and similar kinds of re-grouping may be found necessary when various social and
recreational activities are organized.

Since the kind of grouping we are now discussing takes
place within schools and is the recognized responsibility
of Heads and teachers one might reasonably expect that
parents and the public at large would manifest little concern about its operation. On the contrary, there are features
of internal school organization which give rise to sharp
controversy. Of these the issue of 'streaming' is the one
which at present attracts most attention. This practice
provokes much the same kind of response as does the
segregation of pupils in different types of school : it is both
staunchly championed and bitterly opposed and, again,
educationists and teachers, as well as parents, are to be
found on each side.

It is with the whole array of grouping procedures that
are currently practised or advocated in relation to primary
and secondary education that this book is concerned. In
this introduction we have gained some impression of the
nature and range of the problems involved in assigning
pupils to schools and in organizing their activities inside
their schools.

7

We must now examine in closer detail such evidence as is available to us concerning the operation and consequences of various forms of grouping and the arguments that are put forward for and against their adoption. In the course of this review a number of questions will be raised to which no adequate answers will be provided. This is not so much because the author has elected to adopt guided discovery as a teaching device but rather for two reasons that will become obvious as we proceed.

The first is that in this, as in many other important areas of concern to educators, there is a dearth of adequately mounted and sustained educational research: there are some questions that we cannot answer because we lack the requisite information.

The second is that even if a good deal more effective research were carried out, it could serve only to contribute towards and not fully to supply the answers that we are seeking. Thinking about educational problems always confronts us eventually with the need to make value judgments. If we could be armed with precise knowledge of the full effects of every available grouping procedure we should still have to decide which of them *ought* to be adopted.

Our ultimate objective must be that of developing a rationale on which this kind of decision may be based.

This will involve us in asking questions about the kind of society that we wish to see established and about the extent to which different forms of grouping might be expected to promote or sustain it.

1

The bases of grouping

In a popular programme that ran for many years on BBC
television it was demonstrated that a group of reasonably
intelligent people, when confronted with a complete stran-
ger, could usually discover his profession or occupation
without having to ask him what it was directly. They were
able to do so because there are principles, of which they
were aware, that govern the range of possibilities in this
respect. A small man is unlikely to be in the police force,
one weighing eighteen stone is probably not earning his
living as a jockey, and so forth.

We might illustrate the factors that determine the grouping of children for educational purposes by envisaging the
situation in which a panel was similarly required to discover, concerning a particular child, the school that he is
attending and the kind of course that he is pursuing there.
What kind of data would they need to gather to enable
them to arrive at a solution to this problem? Their task
would be simplified if they drew up a standard form or
questionnaire which required each contestant to supply
information under the following heads:

1   Age and date of birth
2   Home address
3   Sex
4   Race and/or religion

5 Social class (or socio-economic status of parent).
  Indicate school that father attended

6 Ability level. Give details of standardized scores obtained in verbal reasoning tests

7 Special defects or disabilities. Give details, e.g., blind, deaf, maladjusted

8 Special gifts/unusual vocational aspirations.
  State if these have been acknowledged.
  Have your parents agreed that you are destined for a career in, for example, music, ballet, the theatre?

I suggest that, if the panel were equipped with detailed knowledge of the available schools, the information supplied by a questionnaire of this kind would enable them to locate most children fairly accurately.

In other words, in assigning children to schools and, to a lesser extent, to classes or other similar sub-groups within their schools, we have regard to one or more of these eight distinguishing attributes. It should be noted that in some instances they are found to operate interdependently. That is to say, if we elect to use one of these criteria as a basis for grouping we may find that another has become involved, even though this was not necessarily our intention. For example, if we group children in accordance with their measured ability, we achieve a result that is not conspicuously dissimilar from that which would emerge if we adopted social class as our yardstick. We shall encounter further instances of this kind of correlation between attributes that we might have thought were independent.

We must now consider, in turn, these various bases of grouping, but not in the order in which they appeared in our projected questionnaire. Although criticisms have been levelled at the ways in which each of them is employed, there are some that are manifestly more controversial than others. The three that have aroused most opposition—

grouping by sex, social class and ability—will be given extensive treatment in the next chapter.

Age

Chronological age is the most widely used and probably the most generally acceptable basis for educational grouping. It is, of course, the prime means of carrying out the initial task of differentiating between those for whom formal education is to be provided and those who are to be left to their own pursuits. We set the limits of compulsory schooling, at any rate, solely in terms of children's ages.

Unfortunately people grow older in a perfectly regular manner. There are no dramatic overnight manifestations that take place on the anniversary of one's birth. Consequently, setting age-limits for schooling must be a somewhat arbitrary procedure. We would all agree that the pram-borne and the elderly and infirm may be safely excluded. Between these extremes, however, we might with equal justification choose several age-ranges different from the one that we have adopted.

Starting school

The lower limit of this range has been set at the age of five. In this respect we differ from most other countries: children tend to start school at six in the United States and in most European countries, and at seven in Scandinavia. Far from being disturbed by this anomaly, we are at present seeking a viable means of reducing the age of entry still further. We are prompted to do this by the evidence that has been gradually accumulating over the past few decades (the works of Hebb, 1949, and of Piaget, 1952, have been notable pioneering contributions in this respect) which indicates that the 'intelligence' that enables children to profit from the experiences that schooling affords is, to a greater extent than it was once supposed, a function of their early upbringing. We have always known that the best advice we could offer to a child who wished to do well in school was that he should choose his parents carefully. But we used to assume that this was important only because it ensured favourable genetic transmission. We now realize that a child's early home background has an important bearing on his subsequent school career in that it may or may not provide him with the degree and kind of stimulation that is necessary for his adequate intellectual development.

Teachers are able to testify not only to the difference in preparedness that children exhibit when they come to school but also to the disturbing fact that those who are relatively backward at this stage become progressively so as they proceed. Infants' teachers, being required for the most part to deal with excessively large classes, are unable to provide those children who come from the most unfavourable home backgrounds with the remedial attention that they need. In the light of our present knowledge it is reasonable to assume that if these children could be provided with a more stimulating environment in what are now their pre-school years, some of them, at least, would be enabled to derive much greater enjoyment and benefit from their formal education.

There are other handicaps that some children suffer at the outset of their school careers that may be less obvious than scholastic unreadiness but are no less harmful to their future progress and welfare. There is ample evidence to support the view that the range and quality of a young child's social relationships exert an important and perhaps lasting influence on his personality and character. By the age of five some children have already developed attitudes and behavioural tendencies that make it difficult for them either to form satisfactory friendships with others of their own age or to establish good relations with their teachers. This may be regarded as another form of backwardness which is also of a progressive kind and which timely intervention could help to remedy.

There would seem to be a strong case, therefore, for lowering the age at which schooling is made available, and, it is arguable, for giving this priority over other proposed reforms that might be competing for a share of our available resources. The most vulnerable and dependent sections of the community surely call for more consideration than those who are equipped to fend for themselves.

Leaving school

The upper age-limit of compulsory schooling was fixed at fourteen at the end of the first world war and raised to fifteen at the end of the second. In times of relative peace the possibility of raising the school-leaving age is one that we discuss interminably. Our attitude towards this anticipated event is rather like that of a man who believes that a cold bath in the morning would be good for his health but who shrinks from the appalling consequences of taking the plunge.

The arguments that are advanced on behalf of raising the school-leaving age are of two main kinds. Life, we would all agree, is becoming progressively more difficult to contend with and the average fifteen-year-old seems ludicrously ill-equipped to cope with its complexities. It is scarcely necessary to remind the reader of what the world around him is like and we can therefore pass on to the second argument which is concerned more specifically with the need to tackle this problem by means of legislation.

One might suppose that because extended educational facilities are now made freely available and increasing numbers of children are taking advantage of them, there is no need or justification for dragooning the rest. For the most part, however, it is the less able children who seize the opportunity to leave school as soon as they are permitted to do so. It is something of a paradox, this argument runs, that those who stand in greatest need of the benefits of formal education, should receive less of it than their abler colleagues.

Although these arguments command a large measure of support, serious misgivings are expressed whenever the extension of formal schooling appears to be imminent. We might be prepared to dismiss the opposition of the pupils and their parents on the grounds that they lack the foresight which we are prepared to exercise on their behalf. And, similarly, although we cannot afford to dismiss it, we might refuse to be dismayed by the predictable reluctance of the tax-payer to shoulder the additional financial burdens that will be involved.

What must give us pause, however, is the resistance that some teachers offer to this proposal. Some older teachers have reason to remember that our last venture of this kind was not, at the outset at least, an unqualified success. The extension was commonly referred to as 'the extra year' and in some schools it was difficult to decide whether the pupils or their teachers were the more relieved when it came to an end.

When we begin to inquire into the nature of the problems that arose we encounter a basic dilemma which still remains to be resolved. It is a phenomenon familiar enough to the teachers of those children who constitute half our future that it becomes more and more difficult to purvey the school's traditional wares to children as they approach the age of discretion. Before they reach their final year many children have largely abandoned interest in sizeable areas of the school curriculum. If we are to invite them to prolong their stay we must clearly choose between two broad alternatives: we must either replace the present curriculum with activities and pursuits that the pupil will find more congenial or so revise and reconstitute it as to recapture their waning interest.

It is frequently advocated that the traditional curriculum should give way wholly or in part to one that offers some form of vocational training. If such a programme is envisaged in terms of courses related to specific vocations it is likely—such is the current rate of technological advance —to be a preparation for large-scale redundancy. Furthermore most of us would subscribe to the view that preparation for future employment is not the sole or even the most important function of schooling even in its 'extra' years.

It is the second alternative that currently enjoys favour, and under the superintendence of the Schools Council, extensive curricular modifications and developments have been undertaken which, it is hoped, will make the next extension of compulsory schooling a less traumatic experience for the teachers concerned and more beneficial to the pupils than the last one proved to be.

Another possible reason why some senior pupils are unenthusiastic about the prospect of prolonging their schooling may be that they object not so much to the activities in which they are invited to participate as to their having to remain within an institution that also houses children of eleven and twelve years of age. If, it is sometimes maintained, they were to be transferred to one that recognizably accorded to them a more adult status, they might suffer an extended period of education more gladly.

In sum, fixing the terminal point of compulsory education—if we assume that resources can be made available for some extension of its duration—calls for decisions about the kind of provision that can satisfy two criteria that have tended in the past to conflict: it must be something that

15

can justifiably be offered, and it must be cast in a form that will be willingly accepted. And we must also consider the extent to which some re-grouping might be necessary in this regard. Any further period of formal education that we envisage could, conceivably, be viably organized in places other than schools.

Changing schools

It has become our established practice to transfer pupils at various stages in their education career from one type or level of school to another and chronological age, in the main, determines the groupings that emerge as a result. Thus we choose the age of seven as the point at which a child is ready to move from an infants' to a junior school. In some instances this does not involve a transfer from one building to another but rather between sections or departments, but the two are normally recognizably distinct.

The age of seven was chosen for this transition presumably on the grounds that the two stages of education concerned call for different levels of physical and emotional maturity. The infants' school is designed to be an extension of the way of life to which the young child is accustomed within his family. At this stage a young child requires close supervision to guarantee even his physical welfare. And he has to come to terms with the problems involved in sharing activities with other children and with strange adults.

Entering the junior school is a first tentative step into the world at large. Here he will find himself belonging to a considerably larger community and encountering teachers who may not regard tying his shoe-laces as one of their accepted responsibilities.

If the distinctions between these two stages are of the kind that have just been adumbrated, chronological age might seem to be an imperfect index of a child's readiness for transfer from one to the other. The range of individual differences is such that it is conceivable that whereas one child of six may be perfectly capable of adapting himself to a junior school's requirements, another of eight might benefit from an extended infant-school experience. On the other hand the prospect of any form of selection at this stage does not bear scrutiny. The solution would seem to lie in accepting chronological age as an administratively convenient grouping device in this regard, whilst at the same time recognizing and catering for the anomalies to which it will inevitably give rise. This involves arrangements for some overlap between the two stages in terms of organization, curriculum, teaching methods and the qualifications of the staffs. It should be added that we have more nearly achieved a solution along these lines at this point of transfer than at others where comparable problems are to be found.

There is a moment in time when, we are told, it is possible to discern a tide rising in the veins of our youth and this signalizes the need to transfer them from primary to secondary schools. This development takes place when they reach the age of eleven in England and Wales, not until twelve in Scotland, and is delayed until thirteen for those who contract out of the maintained-schools system. These variations indicate that there is a lack of unanimity about the appropriate timing of this transition. The age of eleven was proposed by the Hadow Committee in 1926 at a time when the school-leaving age was fixed at fourteen and there seemed to be no immediate prospect of its being raised. In these circumstances, any later age of entry would have made it impossible to design a viable secondary-school course.

Since these constraints have been removed—we are promised a school-leaving age of sixteen and, moreover, a growing proportion of pupils stay at school beyond this point—it is now open to us to review these arrangements. It might be argued that in opting originally for eleven as the point of transfer we were fortunate enough to choose the right age, although for the wrong reasons. The studies of children's intellectual development that were prompted by Piaget's original work (see Hunt, 1961, Flavell, 1963, and Sigel and Hooper, 1968, for summaries and critical discussions of these investigations) indicate that at about the age of eleven children pass from the stage of 'concrete operations' to that of 'formal operations'. Furthermore, the cognitive activities that are involved at the concrete-operations stage correspond to those for which provision is normally made in our primary schools, whereas it is on formal operations that emphasis begins to be placed from the outset of the secondary-school course.

Neither Piaget, however, nor any of those who have repeated and confirmed his observations, would claim that a child passes smoothly from the concrete to the formal stage during the first week of September following his eleventh birthday. In the restricted sense of being capable of dealing with the kind of work that is regarded as appropriate to the secondary stage some children are ripe for transfer at a considerably earlier age, others by no means prepared at eleven. Clearly, choosing a later age for transfer would not of itself overcome this difficulty. As we saw earlier, it is the kind of problem that can be adequately solved only if arrangements can be made for children to be accorded the kind of educational treatment that is appropriate to their stage of development, irrespective of what their chronological age might be.

An argument that is sometimes advanced against the choice of eleven as the age for transfer to secondary schools is related to the practice that was formerly standard and is still widespread, if less obtrusive, of selecting about a fifth of the children concerned as suitable candidates for a grammar-school education and diverting the remainder to schools of other kinds. The essence of the argument is that eleven is too tender an age at which to carry out a form of discrimination that has such far-reaching consequences. We shall be dealing with this whole question in more detail in the chapter that follows. Here we are concerned only with the notion that as a technical operation selection could be more efficiently conducted if it were delayed for a year or two. There is no evidence to be adduced in support of this case and some that can be brought against it. As we have seen, transfer to secondary schools in Scotland is deferred until children reach the age of twelve. Nevertheless the arrangements for selection in Scotland have been shown to be no more satisfactory, in terms of the apparent errors involved, than those in England and Wales. We have experience too of applying to samples of thirteen-year-olds the same kinds of test as those used in assessing the abilities and attainments of eleven-year-old children. The results do not entitle us to assume that selection carried out at this age would be substantially more valid.

An interesting new grouping pattern is being widely advocated at present and has been introduced in some areas. This involves the establishment of a 'middle' school to cater for children between the ages of nine and thirteen. A number of advantages may be claimed on its behalf. The first is that it can serve to reduce the amount of rebuilding that is required in changing over to a system of comprehensive secondary schools. Such schools, if they are to house all the children from eleven to sixteen and beyond in a given catchment area must inevitably be considerably larger than those that have formerly had to cater for only a proportion of them. By rearranging the age-groupings, however, some of these schools may be designated as middle schools, others as ʳecondary or high schools, and only relatively minor modifications are needed for the reorganization to take effect. A second argument in favour of the middle school is that it serves to bring the maintained-schools system into line with the private sector. The age-range of nine to thirteen is the one for which most preparatory schools cater and, therefore, this arrangement would make inter-change between the two systems possible and might facilitate their eventual integration.

A third possible advantage of this form of grouping is that the middle school comfortably spans the apparently crucial transition that a child has to make from the con-crete to the formal operations stage of his intellectual development. Whether or not we are able to accept Piaget's formulation of the course that this development follows it cannot be denied that our present educational arrangements tend to require children, when they move from primary to secondary schools, to make fairly rapid adjustments. The work to which they are often introduced from the outset of the secondary-school course demands markedly different kinds and levels of intellectual skill than those they have been accustomed to practising. As we know, some are ready to meet these demands; others have still some way to go before they will be adequately equipped to do so. Within a middle school it should be possible to adjust these curricular changes to suit each child's rate of development and to ensure that he encounters teachers who are, by inclination and training, adequate for his purposes. This latter point perhaps deserves to be stressed since it refers to what could well be the single most im-portant advantage of this form of grouping. To illustrate it we might consider the problem of teaching children to read. There can be no more serviceable accomplishment than the ability to read with facility and it is no exaggera-tion to claim that a child's chances of success in a secon-dary-school course largely depend on the level he has reached in this respect. Since we have reason to expect that the majority of children will have acquired this skill by the time they reach the age of eleven, training in the teaching of reading is, in the main, offered only to intending primary-school teachers. Those preparing to teach in secondary schools do not expect to have to undertake this task nor do many of them wish to do so. Consequently such children—and their number is not inconsiderable— who reach the secondary stage still requiring further tuition in reading are rarely, in present circumstances, afforded the skilled treatment that they require and which could well salvage their educational prospects (see Morris, 1966). In a middle school there would be a mixed staff, in the sense that some would have been trained as primary and others as secondary-school teachers, and, therefore, this gap in our present provision could conceivably be filled. On the other side of the coin, it is sometimes alleged that gifted children are insufficiently 'stretched' in their primary schools. If this is a desirable operation the middle school could presumably undertake it. There might well be profit on all sides.

Finally, if it were envisaged that children on entering their secondary schools should be assigned to courses of different kinds, the middle school would provide a means, similar to that employed in the French *cycle d'orientation*, of systematic observation and assessment on which the necessary educational guidance could be based.

Age-groups within schools

In the early part of this century the schools of this country tended to group children in accordance with the standard of their attainments. Indeed the classes in the schools, once the infant stage had been completed, were described as 'standards' and numbered usually from one to seven. At the end of each year pupils were promoted if they had reached a satisfactory level of achievement, kept down in the same class for a further year if they had not. Exceptionally able children were sometimes allowed to miss out one or more standards and thus might reach somewhere near the top of the school at a relatively early age. The consequence of this arrangement was that within any given class there could well be an age-range of two to three years: the majority would be of an age appropriate to their standard; some would be relatively young, having been granted one or more exemptions from service in lower standards; and the remainder would be those elderly citizens who had occupied the same seats for as long as the teacher cared to remember.

This came to be regarded by the teachers concerned as an undesirable practice. Those who had been denied promotion often became poorly motivated and even resentful and those for whom promotion had been rapid were often out of their emotional depth among their older classmates. In the 1930s the policy of grouping by standards or grades was gradually replaced by one which yielded classes drawn from members of a single year-group. Since this time chronological age has been one of the major bases of grouping within schools although the use of other criteria for forming sub-divisions within year-groups has also become widespread.

It is interesting to note, however, that there has been a tendency in recent years towards the re-introduction of classes that contain representatives of two or three year-groups. In some primary schools, for example, 'family groups' have been established for teaching purposes. The rationale for this form of organization is that children, in their homes and immediate neighbourhoods, are accustomed to associating with others in groups that exhibit a somewhat wider range than those that have come to characterize

the classes in our schools. Furthermore, these more heterogeneous groups are seen to offer certain advantages to their
members. Those to be derived by the younger ones are of
course obvious: the company of slightly older children can
serve as an effective stimulus to their development. It is
also claimed that older children can benefit from this
arrangement. Not only does it introduce them to the role
of responsible leadership which can promote their emotional and social development, but it can assist their
scholastic progress. There is perhaps no better way of
consolidating newly acquired knowledge than by trying
to communicate it to another person.

In secondary schools, too, opportunities are provided for
the members of different age-groups to associate for some
of their activities. The house system is a common device
for securing this form of co-operation. For the most part,
however, grouping by chronological age has gained broad
acceptance, being favoured, with the qualifications we have
noted above, by teachers, parents and the pupils themselves.

Home address

The vast majority of the children in this country attend
schools only by day (the proportion housed in schools that
provide boarding is rather less than 6 per cent). An important principle governing inter-school grouping, therefore, is that children should be assigned to schools that
are within reach of their homes and, to this end, the siting
of schools is related to the distribution of the population.
Primary schools, particularly, tend to serve very limited
catchment areas since young children cannot be expected
to undertake sizeable journeys.

One difficulty that arises in applying this principle is
that, over the country as a whole, the population is not

evenly distributed. In densely populated cities the boundaries of areas that were once identifiable as districts or neighbourhoods tend to become indistinct and the definition of school catchment areas is a somewhat arbitrary operation. In such circumstances it may be difficult for a school to develop among its pupils and their parents the sense that it belongs to, and exists to serve, a recognizable community.

In sparsely populated areas, on the other hand, a choice has to be made between providing a number of very small schools each serving a small village, for example, or requiring the children to travel to a larger, centrally sited establishment. Advantages are claimed for each of these alternatives. The small rural school—or at least the somewhat romanticized version of it with which our literature abounds—would seem to provide an almost ideal setting for a child's introduction to formal education. Such a school is an integral part of the life of the community, often serving as a focal point for the social activities of the adults as well as the children. In these circumstances going to school must seem to a child as a natural extension and enrichment of his daily life. He and his companions merely move indoors and carry on an already familiar association, and there can be none of the emotional shocks or threats to security that beset some children when they enter school for the first time. Furthermore, if family grouping confers the advantages that its supporters claim for it, the village school may be held to offer an additional bonus in this respect.

The larger school, serving a wider catchment area, can claim to offer a richer, more varied educational experience than pupils are able to obtain in small village schools. Not only do they have more teachers to deploy but, being less remotely situated, they are able to attract better qualified teachers, some of whom can be employed to perform specialized functions. It is also more feasible to equip such schools with the various aids that are commonly held to be a valuable feature of modern educational methods. The cost of providing small schools with television sets, film projectors, teaching machines and even with the full range of text books that their pupils require is becoming prohibitive.

A comparable choice has to be made in more densely populated areas, particularly with regard to the provision of secondary schools. To serve a given area of a city, for example, two moderately sized schools or one very large one might be regarded as viable alternatives. One argument for the latter is that it can offer a wide variety of courses and so cater effectively for individual differences in educational need. Another is that it enables more economic use of man-power, and this is particularly important when there is an acute shortage of teachers qualified to teach particular subjects. The main argument that is used against the policy of establishing very large schools is that once their total membership exceeds a number as yet unspecified they become impersonal organizations within which close relations between staff and pupils are difficult to foster. This confronts us again with the vexed question of what may be regarded as an optimal size for a school. The collective experience of teachers would seem to confirm that this lies somewhere between 25 and 2,500. Each individual teacher, when questioned on the subject, tends to propose a figure that is found to approximate closely to the size of the school in which he himself has enjoyed the greater part of his professional experience. The answer clearly must depend on the kind of internal organization that is envisaged and on the roles that it is thought proper to assign to the heads of schools and their staffs. If a Head must be able to recognize each of his pupils and instantly call to mind his name and details of his school record, the school has to be limited to 300 or 400 pupils.

If the Head is not required to perform this feat but may delegate the responsibility to some of his assistants, one can entertain the possibility of the size increasing indefinitely with the same degree of oversight guaranteed to each pupil. All that we can say about a limit to this form of expansion is that no convincing demonstration of its having been reached has yet been provided.

One objection that is sometimes brought against this basis of grouping, is that it may conflict with others that are held to be desirable. If, for example, it is considered advantageous to segregate those pupils who manifest an above-average level of ability it may be necessary for the schools concerned to recruit pupils from outside their immediate neighbourhood. Even wider catchment areas need to be defined if schools are to cater specifically for children with unusual attributes or rare disabilities.

Another serious difficulty that may arise if grouping is based solely on proximity is that other forms of grouping may become involved which are not necessarily sought or even approved by those who plan the arrangements. We referred earlier to the fact that some of the bases of grouping that we have identified tend to operate interdependently. For example, in some areas common or neighbourhood secondary schools have been set up expressly to avoid the segregation of pupils in terms of their ability and social class. The intention has been to create school societies that are comprehensive in character, accommodating children of all levels of ability and drawn from widely different social backgrounds. This aim can be fully realized only if the catchment area of each school contains a representative sample of the community as a whole. This condition is often far from satisfied. In many of our large cities some localities have become residential areas for the members of one fairly narrow social stratum and, sometimes, mainly for citizens of one particular race or colour. In these circumstances, grouping on a neighbourhood basis may yield unwanted forms of segregation. Thus in many parts of the country comprehensive schools and neighbourhood schools are far from synonymous terms.

Every child can lay claim to a specific chronological age and, unless he is unusually unfortunate, to a relatively fixed abode. Not every child, however, belongs to a minority group that is distinguishable from the rest of society by virtue of its religious faith, race, language or colour, or because its members manifest unusual needs or disabilities. We must now consider the extent to which these divisions are or ought to be reflected in the arrangements we make for educational grouping.

Religious denomination

If we were concerned with a detailed history of educational grouping rather than with a consideration of current practices in this respect, this topic would call for extensive treatment. And it would provide a record of some of the bitterest controversies that have been associated with the operation of assigning pupils to schools of different kinds. Until the middle of the nineteenth century the churches had played a considerable part in setting up schools and maintaining such as were available. They could justly claim to have been the first in the field. The history of our educational arrangements since that time is one of increasing intervention by the state, and we may characterize our present system as being predominantly publicly provided and secular.

The members of some of the religious denominations, however—notably the Anglicans and Roman Catholics—have fought a stubborn rearguard action against the forces of the state and its local education authorities. The legacy of these struggles to preserve the 'dual system' is a complex array of administrative arrangements whereby certain schools may be accorded a degree of independence and at the same time receive some financial assistance from public funds. For example, a school that had been previously owned and maintained by a church was permitted, by the provisions of the 1944 Education Act, to acquire 'voluntary aided' status. This allows its board of managers, subject to certain conditions, to appoint the staff and to make provision for denominational religious worship and instruction. On its part, the local education authority was prepared to undertake the cost of maintaining the school and to make capital grants of up to 50 per cent of the total cost towards expenditure on rebuilding or structural alterations. Since the 1944 Act there has been a succession of agreements each resulting in an increased share of the capital costs being awarded from public funds. There are at present over 5,000 schools that are substantially supported in this fashion, and which are concerned with the education of children who belong to a particular religious denomination.

Although this basis of grouping no longer gives rise to the passionate disputes that it occasioned during the first half of this century, it is still an issue on which differences of opinion are expressed. Those who support it do so in the name of freedom and the rights of individual parents to have their children brought up in accordance with their fundamental beliefs. The case against it is argued at two levels. There are those who maintain that public money ought not to be spent on a form of education that is designed to inculcate beliefs to which the majority of citizens are opposed. Education of this kind, it is argued, should be paid for entirely by those parents who insist upon it. This is a sordid view and, since it would inevitably lead to some children having to suffer an inferior education, it is not one to which a civilized community could subscribe.

28

Without descending to this uncharitable level, however, and whilst still respecting the views of the parents concerned, one might question the necessity or the wisdom of this form of grouping. As to its necessity, one might point to the signs that are becoming apparent that the demands for this kind of segregation are not nearly as widespread or insistent among the members of the various religious denominations as they once were. In England, at any rate, the numbers of those who are deeply concerned either about their own or their neighbours' religious affiliations is declining rapidly. And among those who still adhere to particular denominations or sects the earlier antagonisms have largely given way to more tolerant attitudes. The progress of the ecumenical movement has had the effect of shifting emphasis from the distinguishing features of the separate divisions of the Church to the common beliefs and purposes that can serve to unite them. As to its wisdom, one might ask whether it is in the interests of society as a whole to separate, during their formative years, children who are distinguishable only by the religious practices and beliefs of their parents. Segregation of this kind might serve to breed the kind of intolerance that we professedly wish to reduce or to eliminate. History, and contemporary events in Northern Ireland, have made us painfully aware of the dreadful consequences to which the more rigid forms of religious sectarianism can lead.

This is not to suggest that all children should be forcibly exposed to the agreed syllabus, but rather that their parents' wishes with regard to religious instruction could conceivably be respected without the need to establish separate schools for this purpose. One can envisage in a large school, at any rate, the possibility of effective arrangements for different kinds of worship and instruction, with the aid, perhaps, of local clergy. The obvious advantage of this alternative would be that the children concerned would be

29

afforded opportunities, during the course of their other activities, of discovering what their counterparts are really like.

Special needs

Local education authorities are required by the Education Act of 1944 to ascertain and to make suitable provision for such children in their areas as suffer from 'any disability of mind or body'. The Act also required the Minister to define the categories of pupils who stand in need of special educational treatment, and in 1959 'The Handicapped Pupils and Special Schools Regulations' stipulated ten distinct groups: those who are blind; partially sighted; deaf; partially hearing; educationally subnormal; epileptic; maladjusted; physically handicapped; suffering from serious speech defects; delicate.

An eleventh category has recently been added to this list, in that, in 1968, the responsibility for children now designated as severely subnormal, and formerly as 'ineducable', was transferred from the Department of Health and Social Security to the Department of Education and Science.

There can be little or no argument about the use of these criteria as bases for inter-school grouping, since the definition of each category precludes the possibility that any child within it is capable of pursuing a course of education in an ordinary school. Indeed it has been expressly stated as the national policy, both in the Education Act of 1944 and in subsequent Departmental circulars dealing with the provision of special education that handicapped children shall be educated in ordinary schools unless the nature or extent of their disability makes this impracticable or undesirable. In the latter regard, consideration needs to be given both to the interests of the handicapped child himself and to those of his school-fellows.

30

Problems arise, however, concerning children who may be regarded as borderline cases for inclusion in some of these categories. The major sensory defects can of course be accurately diagnosed and therefore decisions about whether or not a child's sight or hearing are good enough to enable him to profit from ordinary schooling are not difficult to make. We are on much less sure ground, however, in determining the limits, for example, of educational subnormality and maladjustment. Consequently there is a not inconsiderable number of children on whose behalf we are called upon to choose between a special school or an ordinary school in which suitable provision can be offered.

There are two schools of thought on this issue. When in doubt, some would argue, the safest course to adopt is to send the child to a special school. There he will not only be in an establishment that is specifically equipped and staffed to cater for his needs, but he will be protected from potentially damaging contacts with normal pupils. A backward child, it is often maintained, can become insecure and poorly motivated if he is regularly exposed to comparison with those who are more intellectually advanced.

The contrary case is that, in many instances, special classes in ordinary schools can be as adequately equipped and staffed as the special schools themselves and can afford the degree of protection that backward children require. They offer the further advantage of being free from the ignominy with which special schools are often unfortunately associated. Thus a child's morale may benefit from his attendance at the same school as his neighbours. We know, too, that a child's progress and levels of achievement are to some extent determined by the norms set by those with whom he comes into contact. If relatively backward children associate exclusively with others of their own kind their development may well be impeded on that account. Some limited, informal contact with abler children, even if this is confined to the school playground, may prove a helpful stimulus. Finally, it should be pointed out, the special education offered to educationally subnormal children—and especially to those near the upper limits of this category—is presumably designed to effect some improvement in their status. One might reasonably expect that some of them will recover sufficient lost ground to be able to take their place in an educationally normal group. In this event, a child who is already in an ordinary school can be transferred easily, as and when the time seems to be ripe for such a move. A comparable transfer of a child from a special school could be a sufficiently traumatic experience to thwart the purposes for which it is intended.

Special educational treatment is also sometimes advocated for those who manifest unusual talents as distinct from disabilities. Thus there are schools—but not amongst those that are maintained by local education authorities—that cater for children who exhibit a flair for acting, or the ballet, or who are exceptionally gifted artistically. Such children, of course, require also the full range of educational facilities that the normal schools provide. That their needs should be met and the development of their special gifts encouraged is of course indisputable. What must surely be questioned, however, is the assumption that this can only be effected by setting up special schools for the purpose. As schools become larger and better equipped—which is the current trend—some of them at least should be able to provide the facilities that, for example, even a musical prodigy requires. And before he leaves to enter the academy or conservatoire where he will perfect his techniques he might well have helped to stimulate a good deal of informed interest among those who will later constitute his audience.

2
Allocating pupils to schools— the major issues

In the previous chapter we examined some of the principles that govern the assignment of pupils to schools of different kinds. We noted that there is general agreement that a child's chronological age and the location of his home must be major considerations in this regard—although, in each instance, problems arise concerning the precise way in which these criteria can be most effectively employed; we recognized too that there can be no argument about the need to segregate those pupils who suffer from certain categories of disability or handicap. We found some grounds for disagreement about the practice of establishing separate schools for children of different religious beliefs, but public discussion of this problem is far less acrimonious than was formerly the case. Indeed, in many large maintained secondary schools one nowadays finds, in not inconsiderable numbers, members of those religious denominations who, a generation ago, would not have been sent to a secular school.

We must now examine those bases of inter-school grouping that currently give rise to the sharpest differences of opinion. The first of these is sex, which, in this context, would seem to be a major preoccupation: the choice between single-sex and co-educational schools gives rise to a good deal of uncertainty and misgiving. The second is that of social class: the distinctively British practice of operating two virtually independent educational systems, one freely available and financed from public funds and the other restricted to those who are able to defray the cost from their own resources, is currently a major political issue. The third is ability or scholastic aptitude: the issue here is the extent to which the differences in ability and attainments that children manifest at the time they leave their primary schools justify their allocation to separate schools.

Single-sex schools or co-education

Infants' schools in this country are almost invariably co-educational, junior schools predominantly so. Among the latter the minority that are of the single-sex type tend to be large schools in urban areas. At the secondary stage there is a preponderance of single-sex schools among the older establishments and of co-educational schools among those more recently built. Over all, the two kinds of school are to be found in almost equal proportions. These facts might suggest that there is a trend towards the replacement of single-sex schools with those of the co-educational type. This may be so, but there is evidence to show that it is not a consistent one and that we are still uncertain on this issue. In recent years, for example, in one of two neighbouring areas two single-sex secondary schools were merged to form one co-educational school; in the other a secondary school that had operated as a co-educational school for many years was reorganized into two single-sex schools. It is noteworthy, too, that in each instance the change met with considerable protest from the parents and teachers concerned.

In discussing this problem we need not confine ourselves to examining the arguments that are advanced in support of each alternative. There is a considerable body of relevant evidence to be considered. We shall remind ourselves first of all of what has been discovered about the differences between boys and girls and assess the extent to which these would seem to call for distinct forms of educational treatment. Finally, we shall examine the results of the inquiries that have been undertaken into the relative levels of attainment reached by children in the two types of school.

Differences in abilities and attainments

A considerable volume of research has been devoted to exploring the extent to which males and females differ with respect to intellectual skills. Initially, attempts were made to discover whether or not there were differences in 'intelligence' in favour of one sex or the other. All mental tests, of course, measure the performances that individuals manifest at a given moment and these reflect the interactions that have occurred since birth between initial endowment and subsequent relevant experience. Since the experiences of males and females are unlike in most cultures, one might expect to find some corresponding differences in their test scores. Indeed these have been shown to depend to some extent on the sex of the person who compiles the tests. Psychometrists speak of masculine and feminine items to distinguish between those that favour males and females respectively.

The many surveys that have involved the administration to large groups of tests of 'general' ability—these sample a wide range of intellectual skills and constitute what are often loosely described as intelligence tests—have revealed no significant differences between the mean scores obtained by males and females. One consistent finding, however, is that the spread of the scores is wider among males than females. This means that the former are more likely to show extreme variations from the mean—in both directions.

Although we may generally conclude that males are neither more nor less intelligent than females—using the term of course in the special and restricted sense which equates it with measured performance in tests of general ability or scholastic aptitude—this is not necessarily true of every stage of development through which children progress. At about the age of eleven, for example, and indeed for some years afterwards, girls manifest higher scores than boys in tests of this kind. At about the same stage, girls are also leading strongly in the race towards physical maturity. These two facts combined have persuaded some parents and teachers that towards the end of the primary school course and during the early part of that in the secondary school boys and girls can be more conveniently educated apart. Age for age, during this period girls are brighter and more grown up than their male counterparts and the latter, it is argued, should be protected from the ignominious position in which they are liable to find themselves in mixed classes.

Differences also become apparent when tests designed to measure specific aspects of intellectual ability are applied to groups of boys and girls. We shall refer to those differences that may be regarded as well established in that they have consistently emerged in a variety of studies (Terman and Tyler, 1954; Vernon, 1961).

In tests of verbal fluency, but not in those involving vocabulary and comprehension, girls prove to be superior to boys. They hold the advantage, too, in tests of manual dexterity, rote memory and visual perception. Boys, on the other hand, must be awarded the palm for spatial ability (which enters into some aspects of mathematics and, oddly enough, of dressmaking), problem solving and mechanical ability.

36

These differences are reflected in the relative levels of attainment that boys and girls exhibit in various school subjects. Girls tend to be superior to boys in English generally—although not in foreign languages to any noticeable extent—and particularly in spelling and handwriting. They are more successful too in art and in a wide range of crafts that call for neatness, precision and dexterity.

Boys come into their own in mathematics and science particularly and, to a lesser but still significant extent, in history and geography.

Interests

Although differences in their intellectual abilities, and particularly differences in the rate at which these develop, are commonly advanced as the grounds for according different forms of educational treatment to boys and girls, the case often largely rests on the fact that they do not share the same interests.

Everyday observation is confirmed by research evidence in this respect. The interests of girls tend to be artistic, musical and literary; those of boys are classified under such headings as adventure, scientific and mechanical. More girls than boys of school age are interested in human problems, in social welfare and in caring for small children, the aged and the needy.

Although girls are not averse to physical exercise or even to games of certain kinds, they do not share the average boy's taste for violent exercise, nor are they so fascinated as boys are by the competitive element in sport. Some of these conflicting interests are linked with the differences that have been noted between boys and girls in respect of various personality traits (Erikson, 1963; Sears, 1967). There are two most notable differences. Per-

37

sonality assessments, using a variety of techniques and involving children with a wide age-range, have shown consistently that boys manifest aggression to a much greater degree than do girls. There is a comparably marked difference, but in the reverse direction, with reference to a trait which may be defined as general sensitivity and responsiveness to people.

There is some evidence, too, that would suggest that compared with boys girls are relatively unstable emotionally, less inclined to challenge authority, and more highly motivated to succeed in school work.

Implications for educational practice

We must now consider the extent to which the differences we have noted imply the need to educate boys and girls in separate schools. The first point to make is that there is no distinction to be drawn between the sexes with regard to general ability or scholastic aptitude. In other words, if we are to judge the issue in terms of their relative capacity to achieve any given academic standard, separate schools are not required.

On the other hand, we have noted specific differences that could conceivably call for some curricular adjustments. Boys appear to be more likely than girls to succeed in some subjects and vice versa. There is no evidence here, however, to suggest that either sex betrays a total incapacity for any of the major subjects in the normal curriculum. At most, these differences indicate that, given a choice at some point in their course, boys and girls may well elect somewhat different groups of subjects.

We saw, too, that there is a tendency during a part of the school course for boys to be outpaced. Towards the end of the primary course and at the beginning of the secondary one the girls are in the ascendancy. That this discrepancy provides sufficient grounds for separating the sexes could be argued only if evidence were available to show that boys suffer some setback as a result of their temporary eclipse. No such evidence has been reported. It is feasible to suppose, on the contrary, that this chastening experience exerts a beneficial influence on the formation of their characters.

It is, as we indicated earlier, on the grounds that, particularly at the secondary stage, the interests, attitudes and aspirations of boys and girls become so disparate that the case for separate schools is mainly argued. Although there are parts of the curriculum that they are happy to share, boys and girls begin to require different subjects and amenities. Girls want rooms for needlework and housecraft; boys demand a woodwork room and an engineering shop. They require differently equipped gymnasia. Girls have little or no use for rugby-football pitches but they may require net-ball and tennis courts, and so forth.

When it was standard practice to house secondary-school pupils in moderately sized buildings, it could be convincingly argued that on administrative and economic grounds these contrasting requirements could be most effectively satisfied by providing single-sex schools. By concentrating several hundred girls, for example, in one place, fuller use could be made of such amenities as domestic-science rooms which are expensive to build and to equip. This argument has now lost some of its force. Large schools are now the order of the day (and this applies to selective as well as to comprehensive schools), and it can no longer be regarded as wasteful to equip these with rooms and facilities that are designed to be used by only half of the pupils.

A more fundamental question that should be examined in this respect concerns the extent to which some of the interests and needs that we are discussing are in fact deeply rooted and predominantly determined by the sex of the individuals concerned. We know that a person's wants are of at least two kinds. He is in need of food, for example, because of the way he is physically constituted and there is little we can do to alter this. He may want a particular kind of toothpaste or television programme, on the other hand, rather because he has been persuaded or taught to want it. Anthropologists who have studied child-rearing practices in different cultures, and psychologists who have studied the factors within a culture that help to shape an individual's personality, have furnished a good deal of evidence to show that some of the characteristics that are held to be distinctive of males or females are developed in response to example, expectations and, sometimes, direct instruction. We, as parents and teachers, prescribe roles that we deem appropriate for children to assume and we tend, from the outset, to differentiate between boys and girls in this respect. We have noted that, in our culture, boys tend to be aggressive, adventurous, interested in mechanical contraptions, good at problem-solving, dirty, ill-kempt and inconsiderate. Girls, on the other hand, are sensitive, altruistic, obedient, interested more in people and domestic matters than in manufactured contrivances, and invariably neat and tidy. We know, too, that in the average home boys are encouraged to 'stand up for themselves' against assaults from their peers, are allowed greater freedom to explore the neighbourhood than is normally accorded to their sisters, presented with Meccano sets for Christmas, and encounter a relatively tolerant attitude when they tramp across the kitchen in muddy boots. The reprimand is half-hearted because 'a real boy' is what the parents hope to foster. Girls are given dolls and encouraged to tend them, help mother in the kitchen, and quickly learn to recognize that rough speech and manners and any lack of regard for their personal appearance are likely to put them out of favour.

There is evidence of a more objective kind to support this view. It has been shown, for example, that boys with fathers in the home develop 'masculine' traits earlier and more securely than those who are brought up by a mother alone. Furthermore, within the first group, differences in this respect are seen to depend on the kind of relationship that a boy is able to establish with his father. If this is of an unsatisfactory kind the boy is prone to develop 'feminine' attributes.

If we accept that some, at any rate, of the interests, needs and personal characteristics that we have been discussing are the products of environmental pressures, it is clear that the choice between single-sex and co-educational schools calls for a somewhat different approach from the one that we have adopted earlier. Instead of assuming that the observed differences between boys and girls are part of the natural order and asking ourselves whether or not they justify separate educational treatment, we should be considering the extent to which it is our policy to reinforce these distinctions or perhaps to try to modify them.

Before discussing this issue, however, we must disclose some further evidence which many people consider largely helps to settle it. We have referred to differences between boys and girls with respect to their abilities, interests and personality traits without examining very closely their extent and significance. The first point to make is that many of these differences are relatively slight. A more important point is that the differences within each sex are considerably greater than those between them. This means, to take a specific example, that although we are justified in claiming that boys are better than girls in tests involving mathematical reasoning, the mean difference is too small to have any practical significance and, furthermore, *some* girls are far above the boy's *average* in such tests. The same qualification must be attached to all the differences we have examined. It follows, therefore, that although a given boy or girl may manifest different patterns of ability and interest, two boys selected at random may well prove to be equally dissimilar. At the risk of labouring the point— but it is clearly one that deserves emphasis—we may express its implications in another form: if we were to design a curriculum to suit the typical boy, we should find some boys for whom it was unsuitable—and some girls for whom it was perfectly adequate.

Nevertheless there is still a policy decision to be made. Although the differences between boys' and girls' characteristics have diminished considerably during the course of our discussion, and we can be left in no doubt that the organization of co-education is viable, we have still to decide whether or not it is in the children's or society's best interests to keep them apart. This is largely a question of what distinctive roles we wish to assign to the two sexes and what set of characteristics we should like to see each develop—since it is clear that these can be influenced to some extent by the experiences we organize for them and the norms we establish and approve.

Unfortunately—and at this point the reader might feel sadly let down—it is not altogether clear in which of two possible directions co-education serves to influence development in this respect. We might have thought that if it were our intention to try to ensure that girls would retain those distinctly feminine characteristics which many parents seem to encourage and that boys, correspondingly, should develop the manly virtues, single-sex schools would be the obvious answer. Whereas co-educational schools would seem to make it possible for the differences between the sexes to become less marked and for each to acquire some of the characteristics of the other. Each of these possible lines of development has its supporters. There are some—parents and teachers alike—who are anxious to see the kinds of distinction we have been discussing carefully preserved: they want girls to stay sweet and kind, and boys to be boys. There are others who would prefer to see boys becoming a little more civilized, losing some of their aggression and developing some of the sensitivity towards other people's needs that is more characteristic of girls; at the same time they would be happy if girls could be persuaded to become a little more assertive and venturesome. Which kind of school will best further each of these aims is a question that we cannot as yet answer. There is some evidence to suggest, however, that our initial guess may be the wrong one. Comparisons have been made between single-sex and co-educational schools in terms of the preferences that pupils express when they are invited to choose among the subjects of the school curriculum. There is a pronounced tendency for a larger proportion of boys in co-educational schools to choose the 'hard' or 'masculine' subjects such as mathematics or physics than that of boys in single-sex schools. Correspondingly girls in co-educational schools are more inclined to choose what may be regarded as their kind of work—literature, art, etc. —than their sisters in girls' schools. The implication of this would seem to be that in the presence of the other sex a boy feels a greater need to assert and demonstrate his masculinity than he does when they are not present. And girls, too, manifest a comparable reaction. Our advice to a parent who is anxious for his son to acquire manly attributes might therefore turn out to be, surprisingly enough, that he ought to send him to a co-educational establishment. If he allows him to go to a boys' school he might become interested in poetry and art.

To complicate the issue still further, we might add that if the extensive and difficult research that would be needed to relate school organization to the personal development of pupils were in fact undertaken, we should almost certainly find, if past experience of researches of this kind is any guide, that differences would emerge among schools of the same type. The kind of influence that any school exerts on its pupils' attitudes and characteristics is, in part at least, determined by the qualities of its staff. One could envisage a co-educational school, for example, so constituted and organized as to be capable of producing either of the alternative effects discussed above. Whether boys and girls in co-educational schools become more like each other or become more sharply differentiated is a question that we are not yet in a position to answer; but that each is given a better opportunity to gain some understanding of the other's characteristics than could possibly be available in a single-sex school can scarcely be denied. And many would regard this as the weightiest argument in favour of co-education. However we may choose to formulate the aims of education, we must recognize that one of the purposes of a school is to equip its pupils to cope with the world outside it. This is not only populated by two sexes, but they have to work together and live together, sometimes in very close proximity. Those who teach in co-educational schools—and particularly those who have had experience also of single-sex schools—would seem to be virtually unanimous in claiming that co-education develops in both boys and girls a healthy and serviceable attitude towards each other and that even if it were deficient in other respects—which they do not allow—this would be a sufficient justification for its existence (Dale, 1969).

Since we are living in a permissive age, a passing reference to sex in its more restricted and popular sense might be allowed. There is little doubt that some parents are disposed to favour single-sex schools because they harbour deep and often unacknowledged fears that co-education might well encourage too close an understanding between boys and girls. They fear that their daughters might be corrupted by this experience and that their sons—who, they recognize, will be corrupted in any event—might suffer undue distraction. One can only point out, in this regard, that co-educational schools have been in existence for several generations and, as yet, there have been no reports of orgies in the classrooms or even in sixth-form coffee bars. As for the possibilities of distraction, the occasional glimpse of a shapely thigh might well temporarily divert a boy's attention from his German grammar (one is inclined to hope, for his sake, that it would) but there are many willing to testify that the dark broodings that can preoccupy a youth who rarely sees a member of the opposite sex from one vacation to the next may much more seriously affect his ability to concentrate on academic work (Lambert, 1968).

For many parents, of course, the judgment of a school's adequacy cannot be based solely, or even mainly, perhaps, on the considerations we have been discussing. The acid test is their child's chance of obtaining satisfactory examination results. We must now consider, therefore, the findings of the many investigations that have been carried out into the relative standards of attainment of pupils in single-sex and co-educational schools.

Research into comparative attainments

The major difficulty encountered in comparing the achievements of pupils in single-sex and co-educational schools is that of making due allowance for the influence on the results of factors other than the one we are concerned to examine. This could be readily overcome if, instead of being required to observe rather unobtrusively what is already going on, we were free to interfere with the lives of other people and to set up controlled experiments. The recipe for an experiment that would provide an un-equivocal answer to the question we are asking would be as follows: take a random sample of teachers and pupils; assign them, again in random fashion, to single-sex and co-educational schools in equal proportions; measure the outcome and settle the issue once and for all. This would afford a comparison between groups that were equal in all respects except that one was distributed among single-sex schools, the other among co-educational estab-lishments.

The alternative procedure, and the one we are compelled to follow, is to wait until the teachers and pupils have assembled in these different types of school before we undertake our investigations. This means, in the event, that the two samples will differ significantly with respect to a number of factors that are known to be related to academic attainment—for example, the level of the pupils' abilities and the nature of their home backgrounds. This is because these factors operate selectively in favour of single-sex schools. Even if comparisons are restricted to those schools that are fully maintained by local education authorities, it is commonly found that among those that are long-estab-lished and have acquired considerable prestige in their localities, the majority tend to be of the single-sex kind. Thus in many areas where children are allocated to secon-dary schools on the basis of their estimated aptitudes and where single-sex and co-educational schools exist side by side the former take the 'cream' as the abler pupils are sometimes described. This is particularly true as far as girls are concerned. When parents are offered a choice, as we noted earlier, they may entertain the possibility of co-education for their sons but they usually prefer single-sex schools for their daughters.

We would expect, therefore, that single-sex schools in

general would manifest higher levels of attainment than their co-educational counterparts and that this superiority would be especially marked in the case of girls' schools. The considerable volume of research that has been undertaken in this field not only fails to confirm this expectation, but provides convincing evidence to show that boys fare far better in co-educational schools than in single-sex schools and that girls too, although perhaps to a lesser extent, are more adequately served by the former. These results are based on public examination results over the whole range of subjects for which pupils are entered. Fortunately we need not cite all the relevant studies separately since R. R. Dale of the University of Swansea, who has devoted a considerable part of his professional lifetime to the study of this issue, has collated and summarized the evidence in a series of articles (Dale, 1962 a, 1962 b, 1964). It is noteworthy that in mathematics, particularly, there is considerable and consistent evidence to show that the attainments of girls in co-educational schools is superior to that of girls in single-sex schools (Dale, 1962 b; Husen, 1967).

In sum, there would seem to be little demonstrable need to use sex as a basis for inter-school grouping and, indeed, some educational and social disadvantages in doing so.

The private sector

Special schools for the children of the comparatively rich are a well-established feature of our educational arrangements. We have some 3,000 schools, housing about 7 per cent of the total number of pupils in the country, to which entry is conditional on the payment of fees which, in some instances, are comparable in amount with the net annual income of a substantial proportion of the population. Admittedly there are some parents who would not claim to belong to the upper socio-economic strata but who, by dint of remarkable thrift and self-sacrifice, send their children to independent schools. By and large, however, it is fair to describe the schools in the private sector as being available only to the better-off section of the community.

These schools are varied in character and quality. They have been described as consisting of an inner circle (comprising the celebrated nine investigated by the Clarendon Commission together with those that have since qualified to play against them), an outer circle, and some clever imitations of the real thing. It is not part of our purpose, however, to consider the fine distinctions that are made amongst them by their connoisseurs. Our concern is with the general principle involved in this form of grouping.

It is self-evident that this practice is socially divisive. The Public Schools Commission reported: 'our general conclusion is that independent schools are a divisive influence in society' (Vol. I, 1968), and the Heads of these schools themselves appear to be virtually unanimous in supporting this verdict. They have for many years expressed their concern about the social exclusiveness of their schools and have searched for some viable means of broadening the entry to them.

That a small group of people should wish to isolate themselves from the rest of the community and to bring up their children to follow a distinctive way of life might not of itself be a matter of major concern. The British, in the main, adopt a tolerant attitude towards minorities and even find them endearing if they can be regarded as relatively harmless eccentrics. If a group of flat-earthers chose to set up schools of their own in order to ensure that their children became securely grounded in their beliefs, they might encounter some opposition, particularly from those who are dedicated to enlightenment, but they would probably escape persecution. The independent schools, however, can scarcely expect to be granted this kind of indulgence. They operate in our society as purveyors of privilege and since the overwhelming majority of the population are excluded from the benefits they have to offer, it is not altogether surprising that there should be rumblings of discontent.

This is at present such a contentious and emotionally charged issue that over-simplification is the order of the day. And in such a brief review of it as this it will be difficult for us to avoid falling into the same error. The reader is advised to consult the suggestions for further reading offered at the end of the book and to defer his own judgment for as long as possible.

One difficulty that stands in the way of getting this problem into perspective is that there are several distinct groups of people involved in, or concerned with, the operation of the independent schools, whose views do not necessarily coincide. Such schools have boards of governors charged with the responsibility of maintaining them and determining, in outline, their policy and aims; Heads and staffs whose duty it is to conduct their day-to-day activities; patrons in the shape of parents willing to pay fees in exchange for the satisfaction of the ambitions that they entertain on behalf of their children; former pupils and some other members of the community at large who have specific expectations concerning the role that these schools should assume. On many important issues some of these groups are found to be at variance with each other. It is for this reason that those who attack and defend the independent schools often find themselves at cross-purposes. One might be attacking, for example, the policy —or what one believes to be the policy—of the governors and parents, only to succeed in provoking the Heads and staffs to assume, with some justification, an air of injured innocence. There is a further complication: within some at least of the groups we have identified, marked differences of opinion are manifested concerning the direction in which independent schools should develop in the future. One is sometimes surprised to discover that some of the severest critics of certain aspects of the private sector are to be found within it.

To return to the basic charge that is levelled against the independent schools, the fact that they make it possible for some members of society to purchase privileges for their children cannot be denied. Every enlisted soldier may be said to have a field-marshal's baton in his knapsack, but it is only those who have been to a public school who seem able to locate it. A public school education affords entry to a relatively small, close-knit community populated by useful 'connections'. A boy's chances of entering some at least of the colleges in Oxford and Cambridge, of rising to a position of eminence in some professions, or of joining a board of directors, are considerably enhanced if he has attended, so to speak, an approved school.

A somewhat disingenuous defence of this outcome is that it is by virtue of the excellent education that they provide that the independent schools are able to secure an advantageous status for their pupils. On this point even their most inflexible opponent would be forced to make some concessions. The standard of education sustained in some of these schools compels admiration. And it would be unduly parsimonious to attribute this entirely to their superior facilities and favourable staff-pupil ratios. This would be akin to withholding praise from a man who had run a four-minute mile on the grounds that there was a following wind. This defence is inadequate, however, because the education provided in many maintained schools is also of a conspicuously high standard. There is a considerable overlap, in this respect, between the maintained and the private sector which is by no means reflected in the subsequent distribution of favours.

Perhaps a more convincing argument on behalf of these schools is that they are indeed used to some extent as avenues to a privileged status but cannot themselves be held responsible for this distortion of their true function. We have noted that some at least of those who teach in independent schools share the misgivings to which we are giving expression. Their predominant concern is to provide education of a high quality and so to develop in their pupils a love of godliness and good learning. Furthermore many of them would welcome the opportunity—or so we are regularly assured—to distribute the benefits that a public school education has to confer over a wider social range. There are parents, too, who value these schools highly because they share this same concern for academic excellence. They are content to secure for their children the best education available even if they become relatively impecunious schoolmasters at the end of it (as the children of such parents almost invariably do).

It would be testing credulity beyond its limits, however, if we were asked to believe that all parents, and all governors of public schools, and all those outside who staunchly champion their existence, were prompted by such creditable motives. It is not a denigration of parents in general but rather a description of the kind of society to which we belong to suggest that, in the main, they are less interested in education for its own sake than in its instrumental aims. The metaphor of life as a kind of athletic event in which a few will win prizes, many will earn plaudits for lasting the distance, and unemployment benefits are to be the lot of the hindmost, colours the attitude of most of us. Parents reflect it when they talk of giving their children a good start in life and when, to this end, they assess schools for their potential value as coaching establishments. It is not unnaturally galling for the 93 per cent, who have some fine athletes among them, to learn that some of the contestants will be half way round the course when the starter's pistol is fired. And it is cold comfort to be assured, in these circumstances, that those responsible for positioning them in this way are not altogether happy with the function they are required to perform.

A question of rights

This form of grouping is often defended on the grounds that parents have a right to do the best for their children and any questioning of this right with regard to sending them to fee-charging schools is attributed to such dark motives as envy or doctrinaire interference. But of course no civilized society has ever accorded to parents unlimited rights concerning the ways in which they bring up their children. Society is prepared to interfere, and on rationally justifiable grounds, when a parent's activities are manifestly not in the best interests of the child himself or when they threaten to impinge unfairly on the rights of others. Thus a parent who claimed the right to beat his children regularly and mercilessly, no matter how beneficial he might regard this treatment, would find himself thwarted by the agencies that society has seen fit to set up to protect children against parental excesses. Similarly a father who ordained that a child should spend half the night practising the piano, with the laudable ambition that he might develop into a competent performer, would encounter protests, which would almost certainly be upheld, from those neighbours whose sleep was being disturbed.

It is arguable that a parent's right to send his child to whatever kind of school he chooses can be questioned on both these grounds. If we believe that a parent is behaving so unwisely in this regard as to prejudice his child's chances of securing the kind of education best suited to his needs, we feel entitled to say so. Indeed, in some circumstances, we intervene and invoke legal sanctions to force him to make a more suitable choice. For example, if it is ascertained that a child is suffering from some disability that prevents him from taking full advantage of the facilities of ordinary schooling, we ordain that he must attend a special school. A parent who insists on his rights and claims that he knows what is best for his child would find himself before the courts. There are some who feel that a case could be made for preventing parents from insisting on a form of grouping that effectively deprives their children, during their formative years, of contact with all but a tiny segment of the society to which they belong. Such children might be described as culturally deprived in a very real sense. Some of them, although being groomed ostensibly to occupy responsible positions, remain appallingly ignorant of the way of life followed by the vast majority of their fellow-citizens. The author talked recently with some sixth-formers in a boys' public school who had attained a sufficiently high academic standard to enable them to gain Oxford scholarships but who were unaware that it was possible for boys to enter for 'O'- and 'A'-level examinations in what they chose to describe as 'council' schools. Evidence of this kind leads one to speculate on the extent to which the well-publicized misunderstandings and failure of communication that characterize many of our industrial disputes, may be attributable to the unfortunate effects of the educational isolation that many of those who hold positions of responsibility in our national life have been required to endure.

The ways in which the exercise of a parent's rights to send his child to an independent school impinge on those of others with respect to their children's material prospects have already been discussed. There is also some conflict here in that the resources available for schooling are unfairly distributed between the private and maintained sectors. Of these, teachers are of course the most important: there is a pronounced scarcity of teachers qualified to teach some subjects—science and mathematics for example—and the private sector has a wholly disproportionate share of these. We may now turn to a consideration of the rights to which the public at large might feel justified to lay claim with regard to the way in which the independent schools should be allowed to operate.

The recent reports of the Public Schools Commission have given wide publicity to the fact that many of the schools in the private sector are not wholly independent in a financial sense. The first report (Vol. 1, Ch. 14) provides details of the extent to which independent schools and the parents who use them are in effect subsidized from public funds. For example, local education authorities currently spend five and a half million pounds on independent school fees and it is estimated that such schools derive about nine per cent of their total annual income from this source. The schools also derive considerable benefit from their charitable status, in the way of rate remissions, tax relief on covenanted income and exemption from selective employment tax. Endowment income escapes liability to tax and may be used to reduce the fees, and parents are able, by a number of devices, to avoid paying the full cost of their children's education out of their existing capital or current income. As a consequence the State is, in effect, paying a not inconsiderable sum towards the cost of independent-school education. This alone entitles its citizens to question the ways in which the private sector is organized.

The general public may, however, claim a more fundamental right as a justification for exercising at least some degree of control over the schools that at present operate independently. A nation's schools may be said to reflect the divisions within a society, and may serve to preserve them. They may also be used as a means of modifying the pattern of its social relationships. If the people of this country became committed to the establishment of an open society, characterized by the maximal attainable degree of equality of opportunity, they might well conclude that the independent schools exercise a more subversive influence than they are prepared to tolerate.

The prospects for integration

At various stages in their history the independent schools have appeared to be on the point of extinction. Each time they have contrived to secure a new lease of life. It is not altogether impossible that they will weather the current storms and continue in their familiar ways.

It would seem highly improbable, however, that they will survive the present century in anything like the form we know them. The public at large is itself better educated than it used to be, and consequently more inclined to concern itself with educational policy and organization. It is now being replenished with a rising generation that would appear to be intent on creating its own classless society; and there is a new militancy to be discerned among those who teach in the maintained schools which is likely to increase the pace of educational reform. It would seem to be reasonable to predict, therefore, that in the near future some resolution of this issue will have to be found.

There would seem to be three broad strategies open to us which might be labelled, respectively, the vindictive, the fearlessly radical and the sweetly reasonable.

The vindictive approach involves severing all connections with the independent sector and using every available means to hasten its demise. The recommended tactics are to insist on its financial independence. All the gaps through which public funds are poured, or are allowed to leak, into the private sector would be carefully sealed. Our available resources would then be exclusively devoted to improving the maintained system. We should not turn to the private sector, as we do now, for assistance with the provision of boarding education for those pupils who stand in need of it, but rather extend the facilities that are already publicly provided in this regard. The ultimate objective of this approach would be so to improve the quality of the education offered by maintained schools as to dissuade parents from patronizing the private sector which, thanks to our other measures, would become more and more inordinately expensive. There would be a need also to bring public pressure to bear on those responsible for distributing favours in order to minimize the extent to which those who could still afford to attend independent schools were able to gain undue privileges as a consequence. One might even envisage the introduction of legislation designed to punish any detectable forms of discrimination based on the type of school that a person had attended.

The approach we have described as fearlessly radical involves a take-over of the independent schools, or, at least, of such of them as the maintained system might regard as serviceable. This would mean acquiring the buildings and offering appointments to those staff who are suitably qualified and could be dissuaded from emigrating or taking up market gardening. This would make available to the state and its local education authorities additional amenities which could be used to supplement existing day- and boarding-school provision or to provide sixth-form colleges or colleges of education. This take-over would presumably involve legislation not only to enable the State to acquire the independent schools but also to put an end to fee-charging so that no other schools could be set up, within this country at least, to take their place. The report of the Public Schools Commission (Vol. I, Ch. 5) indicates that there would be 'no intrinsic difficulty' in mounting this operation, nor did they regard it as being, in principle, wrong, either morally or educationally. They rejected it mainly on the grounds that in their view public opinion is not yet ready to support the total abolition of the public schools and that the cost would be considerable. This is estimated as involving, if all independent schools were taken over, additional expenditure of about sixty million pounds a year, but as the report points out, 'this would of course be no more than a marginal addition to the gross national education bill'.

The strategy designated as sweetly reasonable involves steering a middle course. One neither shuns nor embraces the independent schools, but invites them to the conference table where the terms for some closer association between the two sides can be agreed. It is the kind of solution that the staffs of independent schools, if not necessarily their governors or the parents of their pupils, have been advocating for a long time. The independent schools would remain independent but would broaden their entry. The major problems to be solved in reaching agreement along these lines would concern the number of pupils to be assigned to the independent schools and assisted by public funds, and the criteria to be used in determining their selection.

We might briefly consider these three approaches in regard to the principle of grouping that we are examining. There is clearly no guarantee that the first would result in its modification. If the ninety-three per cent set out to harry and persecute the seven, they might succeed only in strengthening the latter's resolve to maintain an independent existence; and since the private sector can count on influential support, its survival, even in these circumstances, is feasible.

The third approach is a compromise which is intended to modify, but not altogether to dispense with, a socially divisive form of grouping. It may be regarded as a first step towards what could eventually become a fully integrated system or, as some have argued, it might be interpreted as an effective means of strengthening the position of the private sector. Behind the smoke-screen created by those schools that accepted a broadened entry, others, it is suggested, could continue their nefarious practices. And the sector as a whole would be economically buttressed by a substantially increased subvention from public funds.

Only the second approach, it would seem—the one for which as yet apparently there is insufficient public support and which would be costly to undertake—would provide a sure and immediate solution.

The reader must be left to reflect for himself on a number of important topics that cannot be treated within the scope of this book. The suggestions for further reading that are to follow will enable him to examine accounts of those distinctive features of public-school education which some regard as sufficient justification for their preservation or which, others would say, could be advantageously imitated by the maintained schools. In particular, he should consider the arguments that are advanced in support of a period of boarding education. The concept of 'boarding need' as a basis of grouping is one that calls for some clarification. There are some obvious candidates for boarding education —orphans and children whose parents are living abroad, for example. It is sometimes maintained, however, that nearly all children would benefit from one or more short periods of residential schooling.

Ability and aptitude

It is to be assumed that the reader has some familiarity with the major trends in our recent educational history and that, therefore, only a passing reference need be made to them in introducing the vexed question of assigning pupils to schools of different kinds on the basis of their levels of ability. During the first half of this century there was a gradual extension of secondary education in response to a growing demand that it should be accorded to all children. A series of commissions were set up to consider if, when and how this reform might be implemented. The Hadow Committee in 1926 gave its approval to the notion, suggesting that the transition from primary to secondary education should occur when children reached the age of eleven. The Spens Committee advised in 1938 that three kinds of schools would be called for if secondary education were to be offered to everyone. The Norwood Committee in 1943 discovered that, conveniently enough, there were three distinct types of children waiting to be distributed among the schools of the tripartite system, as it came to be called. The culminating point of all this endeavour was the Education Act of 1944, which created the framework within which a system of secondary education for all pupils could be developed and enjoined local education authorities to furnish the children under their care with a form of education suited to their ages, abilities and aptitudes.

The notion, implicit in the 1944 Act, but made explicit in the reports that preceded it and in subsequent Ministry circulars, that children of different levels of ability and aptitude need to be segregated during the period of their secondary schooling, is the one that we are to examine in this section. It calls for examination because it is still a controversial issue. Although many local education authorities have abandoned the practice of grouping primary-school leavers according to their estimated abilities, there are some who appear to be intent on retaining it. There is some advocacy, too, for a wholesale reversion to selection for different types of secondary school as a standard procedure. There is a good deal of evidence available to us concerning the operation and consequences of this form of grouping; and an increasing amount, too, on the results that emerge when it is not practised.

The process of selection

The selection of pupils for entry to different types of secondary school involves some assessment of those abilities that are regarded as serviceable predictors of success in academic courses of a demanding character. We know a good deal about these abilities and their measurement. The first point to emphasize in this regard is that their distribution assumes a continuous form. That is to say, if we examine the test results of a large representative sample of children, we find that the whole range of scores is occupied. There are no gaps along the continuum which would enable us to distinguish particular groups. Measurements of some other attributes such as, for example, height, also display this form of distribution. Let us suppose that we were required to provide schools for tall children and others, of a different kind, for those considered small. Of course everybody can recognize a tall child when he sees one, and, in certain instances, we should have little difficulty in assigning pupils on this basis. We should reach a point, however, as we moved down the scale, when we become uncertain as to whether a given child could be regarded as quite tall enough for our purposes. And we would find that the difference between his height and that of the last one to be admitted was not discernible to the naked eye.

It is this kind of problem that confronts us when we try to distinguish between those children who are and those who are not suitable for a grammar school education. The dividing line, wherever we choose to draw it, separates two children between whose levels of ability it is virtually impossible to discriminate. Honesty compels us therefore to admit to the children concerned and to their parents that our decisions in this respect are essentially arbitrary. And if these decisions matter—if for example a child and his parents have reason to regard a grammar school as preferable to the alternative that may be offered—we may well be accused of being less than sensible or just in operating a system of this kind.

We have just considered the case of two children, indistinguishable in terms of their measured abilities, one of whom has been selected for a grammar school, the other rejected, and we have recognized that this is an inevitable consequence of the fact that abilities are distributed in a continuous fashion. We can well imagine that the rejected child and his parents would be even more deeply incensed if they were to discover that the measurements on which this arbitrary decision is based are themselves unreliable and that if either a different test had been used, or the same test had been administered at a different time, it is distinctly probable that the relative positions of the two children would have been reversed. This unreliability is characteristic of whatever means of assessment we adopt. The standardized objective tests that were used in the eleven-plus examination—and still are in those areas where selection continues to flourish—were adopted for this purpose because their reliability is higher than that of alternative forms of assessment and the degree of error to which they are prone can, moreover, be ascertained. Even these tests, however, provide an indication only of the fairly wide range of scores within which a child's 'true' score may be expected to fall. Thus if a child obtained a score of, say, 115, all that we are entitled to conclude is that the score which reflects his real level of ability lies somewhere between 109 and 121 (Pidgeon and Yates, 1968). It is on the basis of these extremely rough indications that selectors are required to undertake their fine discriminations.

These considerations would lead us to expect that predictions based on measurements of this kind would prove to be of limited value. We need not speculate on this issue, however, because the results of a number of carefully controlled follow-up studies are available to us. (References to these will be found in the suggestions for further reading.) These studies involved assessments of the progress and achievements of pupils in secondary schools of various kinds. These assessments were then compared with the predictions that could be afforded by the whole array of available test scores, examination results and primary-school teachers' estimates in respect of these pupils at the outset of their course. These investigations enable us to evaluate, with some accuracy, the validity of such selection procedures as have been so far devised. They show that the most successful methods of selection, involving a combination of teachers' assessments, batteries of standardized tests, procedures for dealing with border-zone candidates, and an array of sophisticated techniques for dealing with the measures that all these provide, lead to errors of allocation affecting one in every ten of the children concerned. Procedures of this kind were extremely costly and time-consuming and not every education authority was able to undertake them. The less elaborate methods that many authorities employed—and some still do—involve an even greater measure of error. Perhaps a more telling way of indicating the size of this problem is to compute, on the basis of the ascertained predictive value of methods of selection at eleven, the percentage of an age-group that would have to be admitted to a grammar school, to ensure that by the time they reached the age of fifteen we could be fairly certain that we had in fact included the top 20 per cent, in terms of their measured abilities. The answer is that to satisfy this condition (and presumably this was the object of the exercise—to ensure that the academically able minority is given a chance to work for 'O'- and 'A'-levels) we should have to admit nearly 70 per cent of the eleven-year-old age group.

These errors of prediction are attributable not only to the imperfections inherent in the methods of assessment that are available to us but also to the fact that children, having been arranged in some sort of order of merit, refuse to stay in their places. Even if we could be certain that we had accurately ascertained the relative levels of ability of a group of eleven-year-olds we should find that a year or two later various events had supervened to modify the initial rank order. Children develop at different rates (we might, at the eleven-plus stage, have compared two children, one at the end of a spurt of development, the other at its outset, and, consequently, discover within a relatively short period that we have misjudged their capacities); their progress is affected in countless small ways and some large ones by their family circumstances (the career of one apparently promising child may be blighted by bereavement or the divorce of his parents: that of another may take a dramatic turn for the better as a result of the resolution of some domestic difficulty that had impeded his earlier progress); their school work may at various times begin to improve or to deteriorate as a consequence of the kinds of relationship they form with the teachers they encounter. These and many other unforeseeable influences help to determine the extent to which they succeed in a particular school or course. We should need the help of a crystal ball to forecast this satisfactorily. We ought to remind ourselves, too, of some of the unfortunate side effects of the selective practices. Widespread parental anxiety communicates itself to the children concerned and, as primary-school teachers can testify, some of these become emotionally disturbed as a consequence. The notorious 'back-wash' effect of the eleven-plus procedure on the life and work of the primary schools has been well documented. Time and energy that could be devoted to creative pursuits and worthwhile educational activities were diverted to the grim grind of cramming and to fostering in young children a high degree of examination craft. Outside the schools a flourishing coaching industry developed and many hapless parents put themselves to considerable expense in order to provide their children with opportunities to continue, during the evenings, the soulless activities that occupied them for the greater part of each day.

This is old information and one might have thought that it was unnecessary to recapitulate it. It would seem, however, that support is gathering for the retention of a selective system in those areas in which it has not yet been abandoned, and even for its reinstatement in some that have begun to develop comprehensive arrangements. In these circumstances, it may be useful to remind ourselves that the wealth of evidence that is available to us concerning the operation of selective procedures demonstrates unequivocally that they not only contribute substantially to the sum of human misery but that they are also manifestly incapable of achieving the objectives for which they are intended.

Reference should also be made to a curious myth to which we are currently invited to lend credence. This is that it is possible to operate a selective system—for example, to maintain a grammar school that admits only a minority of the children within its catchment area—without, however, involving ourselves in the difficulties and embarrassments that we have just been considering. That the 'eleven-plus' can be abolished, but, at the same time, grammar schools may be preserved, is a proposition that is nowadays being seriously entertained. One can envisage, of course, the possibility of grammar schools and

64

comprehensive schools existing side by side, as it were, in the sense that a county, for example, may be divided into distinct areas, in one of which a selective system operates, and in the other one of a comprehensive kind. The viability of an organization of this kind depends on the extent to which the parents and teachers in each area can be persuaded to accept the arrangements that are offered. It is sometimes suggested, however, that within a given area, the eleven-plus can be abandoned and, notwithstanding, a grammar school can still be provided with an appropriate intake of pupils. What those who entertain this possibility presumably have in mind is that one may remove the familiar panoply of the selection procedure—formal examinations, tests, interviews for border-zone candidates and the like—and leave the selection of candidates for the grammar school to the judgment of primary-school teachers. It is important that we should be clear about what this proposal involves. All the evidence that has been accumulated on this issue consistently demonstrates that this device would serve to increase, and to a significant extent, the number of misplacements. The abolition of the eleven-plus examination, in this sense, means, in effect, the substitution of a less reliable and less valid procedure. The follow-up studies that have examined the effects of methods of selection, and to which reference is made in the suggestions for further reading, show that the most successful predictions (and, as we have seen, these leave much to be desired) rely on a combination of primary teachers' assessments and a whole array of other measures. If either of these major components is used alone, the procedure becomes demonstrably less efficient and, therefore, less just.

The consequences of abandoning selection

We have considered the difficulties involved in attempting to operate a selective system, the anxiety that it provokes in parents, the injustice that it does to many children and the blight it casts on the life and work of primary schools. We must now inquire into what is likely to happen if we abandon the attempt. Does this bring in its train consequences of a different but equally unfortunate kind? If this were the case we would be faced with the distasteful problem of choosing between two evils.

If we forgo selection altogether, we have to reorganize secondary education along comprehensive lines and develop schools capable of satisfying the educational needs of children of all levels of ability and aptitude. We are making faltering progress in this direction, with the approval, it would seem, of the majority of parents and teachers. There are some, however, who express grave misgivings concerning the possible outcome of this reorganization. Although objections are levelled against comprehensive schools on a number of grounds, the major argument—and the crucial issue for us to examine—is that they will not provide, for the abler minority of pupils, as stimulating and supportive an environment as that afforded by grammar schools and that, therefore, they will be responsible for a lowering of academic standards. This point of view is crystallized in expressions such as 'levelling down', 'more means worse' and 'dilution', which are familiar echoes of the debates that have centred around this issue in recent years. But before we began to set up comprehensive schools in earnest, evidence was becoming available that served to call into question the assumption that the kind of course offered by grammar schools can be successfully pursued by only a small minority of pupils. (We were never altogether sure, of course, about the size of this minority, nor about the attributes that define a grammar-school course: the 'standards' that grammar schools regarded as appropriate varied considerably from one to another.) An inquiry instituted by the Advisory Council for Education (Early Leaving 1954) examined, for example, the attainments in public examinations of schools which adopted markedly different policies with regard to the proportion of the children in their areas that were granted admission. In the sample of schools selected for investigation this ranged from approximately ten to forty per cent of the available primary school leavers. The first point to make about these differences is that they were shown not to reflect comparable variations in the levels of ability manifested by the children in the areas concerned; they were related rather to differences in policy regarding selection for grammar schools or in the number of places that could be made available in such schools. The result of the inquiry ran counter to expectation. One would have supposed that a school with a highly selective intake of pupils would obtain results markedly superior to those shown by a school that cast its net far wider. In the event, it was found that the proportion of successes was roughly comparable from school to school, in spite of the fact that some had practised 'dilution' to a considerable degree. More did not prove to be worse: the high-fliers continued to soar and some of those who, in other circumstances, would have been denied the opportunity to follow a grammar-school course proved that they were capable of profiting from it.

Another development which yielded evidence of the same kind began in the 1950s. The rigid divisions of the tripartite system were seen by the teachers on the classroom floor to be less than satisfactory. Finding that, contrary to the apparent indications of the selection procedure, some of their pupils had both a pronounced taste and capacity for academic pursuits, the teachers in secondary-modern schools began to press for and were eventually allowed to provide courses leading to 'O'-level and beyond. Again it was demonstrated that, whatever selection ratio had been adopted in a particular area, candidates could be found for the academic courses instituted by its secondary-modern schools.

These findings gave added impetus to the trend that was already developing towards the setting up of secondary schools of a comprehensive kind. Whenever these have been introduced the outcome that we have noted has become apparent—that is, there has been a significant increase in the proportion of children found able and willing to achieve the kind of academic success that used to be regarded as the prerogative of a selected minority (Pedley, 1963). The public schools have always known this of course and many of them—even some of the famous ones—have been far less selective with regard to their entrants' abilities, than have the maintained grammar schools. Evidence of this, and of the fact that eleven-plus 'failures' are capable of achieving academic success has been furnished by the Head of Marlborough College (Dancy, 1963).

It must be admitted, of course, that the kind of evidence we have been considering fails to answer our initial question, which concerned the extent to which the brightest children might find their progress hampered if they were all to be educated in comprehensive schools. All that we have shown, it might be objected, is that such a form of organization will improve the prospects of considerable numbers of children who fall outside this category.

For obvious reasons, there is little direct evidence on this point to be found within this country—and it is the British habit to regard the experience of foreigners as of doubtful relevance to our concerns. We have little evidence because experiment is virtually impossible: we cannot envisage assigning pupils at random to schools of different kinds in order to assess the outcome. We are forced, therefore, to try to draw inferences from observations that we can make in the situation as we find it. And the situation as we find it largely precludes direct comparisons of the kind we require. Although we have a sizeable number of comprehensive schools, relatively few of them are so situated as to be able to admit, from a reasonably representative catchment area, all the pupils who require secondary education. Many of them are in direct competition with grammar schools or direct-grant schools and are thus deprived of many of those children in whose progress we are interested. In these circumstances, research has been able only to nibble round the edges of the problem. What can be asserted about the studies that have so far been undertaken—these are scattered round the journals and too numerous to cite—is that they furnish no evidence in support of the view that the progress of able children is affected by their association (to the extent of sharing the same building, that is) with children of lesser ability. They provide strongly suggestive evidence that the latter benefit considerably from this arrangement. It must be admitted, however, that if we are to rely only on our domestic supply of research evidence we cannot expect a definitive answer to this question for some considerable time.

If, however, we are prepared to consider evidence from other countries, we can draw somewhat firmer conclusions. As soon as we examine the education systems that are in operation elsewhere, the faith that we have placed in selection and segregation begins inevitably to be shaken. It is surely open to question that our educational achievements, whatever criteria we may choose to adopt for their evaluation, are markedly superior to those manifested in countries where these practices are avoided. For some years now a large-scale, carefully controlled investigation has been conducted (the International Project for the Evaluation of Educational Achievement (IEA)) which is designed to compare the outcomes of different forms of school organization and educational practice. An initial report has already been published (Husen, 1967) and further reports are in preparation. The evidence from this source amply confirms the predictions of those who advocate the establishment of common or comprehensive schools. It shows that in such schools the standards of the ablest children are not adversely affected and, moreover, that the total 'yield' in terms of the numbers of pupils who reach those levels of attainment that we have been prone to regard as within the compass of only a small minority is significantly increased.

Apart from these comparative studies, investigations carried out within a number of countries have furnished comparable results (Yates, 1966). Special mention must be made of Sweden in this regard. There the change-over from a selective to a comprehensive system has been closely observed and documented (Svenson, 1962; Husen and Svenson, 1960), and cumulative evidence of a remarkably consistent kind testifies to the advantages that have accrued from this transition.

Even the most cautious interpretation of the available evidence would seem to support the hypothesis that there is little to be lost and much to be gained by abandoning the practice of inter-school grouping on the basis of pupils' initial abilities.

3
Grouping within schools

General features

In most schools, and particularly in large secondary schools, it is found necessary to undertake a series of grouping operations in order to organize the varied activities in which it is considered appropriate that pupils and teachers should take part. Even the one-teacher, one-room village school rarely functions as a single undifferentiated group: for various purposes the teacher tends to identify distinct sections of pupils and to assign them to different corners or spaces. In a large school there is usually a form of coarse grouping involved which may be regarded as preliminary to, or sometimes independent of, that which is designed to establish classes or instructional units. In the interests of administrative convenience there is a need to separate a large school's population into a number of manageable divisions. There is a limit to the number of pupils on whose behalf a single individual can perform the requisite desk-work—compiling records, filling in forms, dealing with correspondence and so forth. In the interests of the pupils, too, it is desirable that they should belong to a group that can be adequately organized in the sense that each has a reasonable chance of being known and appreciated as an individual. It is also, therefore, in order to ensure that adequate pastoral care can be exercised, that a large school's population calls for some sub-division.

Two broad approaches to this form of grouping may be distinguished: these have been characterized as 'horizontal' and 'vertical' grouping. These epithets refer to the notional boundaries between the sub-divisions that might be created in a large school. We tend to think of children moving 'upwards' in a school. The bottom of the school is the point of entry and as a child grows older he approaches the top of the school. If we represent this conception in diagrammatic form, any horizontal lines drawn across it will form groups that are distinguishable from each other in terms of chronological age. If, on the other hand, the rectangle that serves to represent the total school population advancing on a broad front from the bottom of the school to the top, is sub-divided by means of vertical lines, we shall create divisions that contain within them pupils of every age—and, indeed, each of the groups so formed may constitute a representative sample of the school as a whole.

Horizontal grouping may be used to form two or more broad divisions which serve as schools within schools. Thus a school housing pupils from the ages of eleven to eighteen may be divided into junior and senior departments, or perhaps into three, with a distinctive middle school. A department created in this fashion may, under the direction of one supervisor, constitute a single administrative unit; or there may be a further overt sub-division into separate year-groups, each with its designated teacher in charge.

Vertical grouping results in the formation of 'houses' or of tutorial groups. The concept of a house within a school originated, of course, in the independent boarding schools where the pupils tend to be divided into groups, each of which lives together in a separate building, superintended by a house master and his own staff. Such houses are not only distinct in a physical sense but serve as the major focal point of a boy's interests and loyalties throughout his school life. When day schools first adopted this form of organization it was, inevitably, in a considerably modified form. In most such schools 'houses' have served administrative and social purposes in the main. They provided, for example, a convenient means of organizing sporting and other forms of competition within the school. In some circumstances they engender among the pupils loyalties and attachments comparable with those manifested by pupils in boarding schools; in others they have proved to be purely formal divisions to which many of those concerned did not attach any particular significance. As schools have grown larger, however, the division into separate houses is seen to be a more necessary and serviceable form of organization. In some of the new purpose-built comprehensive schools, for example, the original conception of a school divided into physically separate houses each with its own dining-rooms and facilities for assembly and association has been re-introduced. In these schools the house is no longer a purely notional division, nor does it serve administrative purposes only, but has its part to play in the organization of a wide range of educational activities.

Another form of vertical grouping (but not necessarily so—this arrangement can be made within the horizontal pattern) involves assigning a number of pupils to a particular member of the staff whose responsibility it is to guide their progress throughout their school careers. Tutor groups of this kind may be formed within houses or may be organized without reference to house divisions.

The National Foundation for Educational Research began an investigation into comprehensive education in 1966 which has involved a close study of the organization of such schools. A preliminary report has been published (Monks, 1968) in which a wealth of detailed information concerning their grouping practices has been made available. Of the 331 schools that were involved in the Founda-

73

tion's survey, it was found that 299 were divided into
separate houses. Most of these contained between 150 and
200 children and the number of houses in a school ranged
from three to ten, depending, of course, on the size of its
enrolment. Almost exactly one-third of the schools, 112
in number, used a horizontal form of grouping and 60 of
them were divided into lower, middle and upper schools.
It will be seen from these totals that vertical and horizontal
forms of grouping are by no means exclusive. If we revert
to our imaginary diagram we can recognize that grouping
in many schools involves drawing lines in both these directions, thus creating cells, as it were, which are regarded as
belonging to the rows for one purpose and to the columns
for another. The survey also showed that 113 of the schools
—again almost exactly one-third—had set up tutor groups
each consisting, on average, of between twenty and thirty
pupils. These arrangements showed a roughly equal division between tutor groups containing pupils of all ages and
those composed of the members of one year-group only.
Although we have a good deal of information about the
practices that schools currently adopt in this regard we
have little or no evidence concerning their relative effectiveness. There are some schools committed to a predominantly vertical form of grouping; some that favour divisions
of a horizontal kind; and many that find it necessary or
convenient to combine the two. There would seem to be a
situation here that calls for empirical research, designed
to compare the outcome of different patterns of organization. Various hypotheses have been advanced in favour of
both vertical and horizontal grouping. The arguments in
favour of vertical grouping are somewhat similar to those
that are advanced for the smaller-scale version of this kind
of organization which is gaining favour in some primary
schools, where it is described as family grouping. The
opportunity for pupils of different ages to meet and to

share some of their activities, is held to offer benefits to juniors and seniors alike. An effective house system—and certain other forms of vertical grouping such as clubs and societies—can bring together in a purposeful way those who in their day-to-day scholastic work are almost inevitably kept apart. It affords to the older pupils a chance to develop qualities of responsible leadership and it can serve to motivate younger pupils to try to emulate the achievements of those whose relative maturity they find impressive and challenging.

The major argument on behalf of horizontal grouping is that the total age-range of a secondary school, particularly if it runs from eleven to eighteen, is far from homogeneous. Within this total assembly it is possible to identify groups that are so distinctive with regard to their educational and social needs as to require a degree of isolation from the rest. They need teachers, for example, who understand and are adequately trained to satisfy these needs, and an opportunity not only to work alongside their peers but also to pursue their recreations without being forced to mix with others who are at a different stage of development and, therefore, do not share their interests. The sharpest contrast, clearly, is that between the fifth- and sixth-formers who are approaching adult status, and the first- and second-year pupils who are only just entering the adolescent phase. These two groups can be expected to co-operate to only a limited extent and require therefore at least partially distinct forms of organization. All schools recognize this, of course. They differ, however, with regard to the boundaries that are chosen to separate pupils of different ages (some, for example, are content to distinguish broadly between juniors and seniors, others introduce a separate middle group) and with regard to the emphasis that is placed on these distinctions (whether, for instance, the divisions that are created should involve simply differences of title and status, or administrative separation as happens when a junior department, say, has its own Head and staff). As we saw in Chapter 1, these differences of view enter into the arguments concerning the ways in which schools themselves should be constituted. There is advocacy, for example, for sixth-form colleges which would cater for some of the more senior pupils who are now housed within secondary schools, and also for middle schools composed of pupils from nine to thirteen, which would relieve secondary schools of their junior members.

Our review of current practices in schools indicates that in a substantial number of them vertical and horizontal grouping are, in various ways, combined. No doubt this is because both the kinds of argument we have outlined above are regarded as having some substance and schools, therefore, are sensibly trying to get the best of both worlds. Of the various patterns available, however, it is conceivable that one might prove to be more effective than another and we would be wise to encourage some relevant research into this problem.

The kind of grouping that in any school, whether large or small, is concerned with the pupils' scholastic activities, involves assigning pupils to classes which still remain the basic units of educational organization. Classes, of course, are not necessarily stable features of a school's grouping arrangements. They may be dispersed and reconstituted several times a day at the sound of a bell. But in the vast majority of schools and for the greater part of the time pupils are to be found in groups ranging usually from twenty to forty, each in the charge of a teacher. The composition of these groups is a sharply controversial issue. But before we address our attention to this problem we must consider two forms of grouping that are in a sense intermediate between the administrative devices we have just been considering and those that determine the contents of a school's working time-table: the formation of separate academic departments and the organization of team teaching.

Departmental organization

In nearly all secondary schools, and to a much more limited extent in some large primary schools, teachers are grouped in separate departments. The basis of this form of grouping are the specialist qualifications of the members of the staff. Those who teach a major subject will usually have a department of their own; others may belong to a department concerned with a number of associated subjects. There will normally be a head of each department who assumes a considerable degree of responsibility for determining, with respect to his subject, the syllabuses and methods of teaching to be used throughout the school. Although this is a form of grouping that concerns teachers only and does not affect pupils directly, it is nevertheless seen to have a bearing on the latter's scholastic development (Michelson, 1967). It is a form of organization that serves to place emphasis on the differences between teachers rather than on their common purpose, and on the distinguishing attributes of subjects rather than on their relatedness. In some schools, departments are rigidly separated and self-contained: not infrequently, the lay-out of the buildings serves to keep various sections of the staff from each other and one finds, for example, that it may be more convenient for the members of the science departments to spend their free time in their own quarters rather than in the staff common rooms. When departments are markedly distinct and, as sometimes happens, develop competitive attitudes towards each other, it is scarcely surprising that pupils should become afflicted with 'subject-mindedness' and that their knowledge should resemble a patch-work quilt rather than a seamless robe. Various counter measures have been proposed to offset the unfortunate effects of this kind of compartmentalization: the development of 'core' curricula; the use of projects; making provision for the 'correlation' of subject syllabuses. The introduction of 'team teaching' is also intended to help in this direction although it is designed also to serve a number of other purposes and involves, moreover, a modified grouping pattern as far as pupils are concerned.

Team teaching

For those who have embraced team teaching it is not so much a form of grouping, more a way of life. Although educational innovations generally may rely on a degree of enthusiastic support, at least for a time (the most effective tonic for a jaded teacher would seem to be a change of method or syllabus), team teaching appears to arouse enthusiasm to an unusual extent. In its most elaborate form it involves a group of teachers representing a number of related or relatable disciplines, who become jointly responsible for planning and conducting the educational activities of a relatively large number of pupils. For example, a team of six teachers, assisted desirably by one or two student-teachers and a clerk, might superintend 200 pupils. Several advantages are claimed on behalf of this form of organization (Shaplin and Olds, 1964). It enables an experienced teacher to spread his influence more widely than if he worked in isolation. (To some extent, of course, the departmental kind of organization may serve this purpose.) It provides a high degree of correlation among the various subjects and disciplines involved, since the whole curricular area for which the team is responsible is jointly planned. It permits of more flexible grouping arrangements as far as the pupils are concerned: they may be assembled in a large group for an inspirational lecture, film or demonstration; whilst the majority are thus engaged it is possible for others to meet in small seminars or for individual tutorials with a member of the teaching team. Thus, it is suggested, grouping may be determined in accordance with the pupils' needs and to suit the particular activities on which they are engaged. It also makes it possible for a teacher to specialize not only in terms of subject-matter but also with regard to methods of instruction. One may be at his most effective in dealing with large groups and broad themes; another may be most successful in conducting small seminars; yet another may have a flair for back-room organization: devising and producing teaching materials and aids of various kinds. Each may be given an opportunity to bid from his strongest suit. A good deal of research has been devoted to team teaching but much of it has been poorly designed and inconclusive. There is some evidence however of positive effects on pupils' achievements and attitudes (Bair and Woodward, 1964).

We must now consider the issues involved in assigning children to separate classes within a school. An examination of this problem involves us in a kind of *déjà vu* experience: having exhausted the topic of selection for different kinds of school, we find ourselves again confronted with the same kinds of argument concerning the need to group pupils within schools on the basis of their abilities and attainments. It is perhaps to be expected that this question arises in primary schools and in comprehensive secondary schools, both of which set out to cater for pupils of every kind; somewhat more surprising that it should be encountered in schools that admit only a selected minority.

Streaming and setting

At present the majority of schools of all kinds base their allocation of pupils to classes, to some extent, on an assessment of their abilities or attainments. And, indeed, in spite of a growing amount of criticism levelled against it by parents and teachers alike, the favoured practice is still that of 'streaming'. This involves the relatively permanent segregation of pupils of different levels of ability : on entry to the school children are assigned to the stream or track that is deemed appropriate and for the most part remain within it for the remainder of their school career.

This practice was familiar in the older grammar-school foundations and in some public schools, but became a feature of primary-school organization as a result of the recommendations of the Primary School Report of 1931. Until then, as we saw earlier, primary schools grouped their pupils in grades or 'standards'. This report advocated that children entering junior schools should be organized in homogeneous classes : the ablest minority were to form the 'A' stream, and their numbers kept small enough to enable them to be adequately prepared for the selection procedure when they reached the age of eleven; the 'C'-stream children, those who were found to be the least able, were also to be placed in small classes so that they could be given appropriate remedial attention; the normal, ordinary average children of the 'B' stream could be taught in sizeable classes if necessary.

Those who support the policy of streaming perceive it as a means of providing for each child the kind of educational environment that is most conducive to his development. In the challenging atmosphere of an 'A' class an able child will be afforded the degree of stimulation that he needs if he is to realize his full potential; if he is hampered by the presence of duller children and so prevented from progressing at the rapid pace that he finds congenial, he may well become frustrated and begin to manifest behavioural problems. In the 'C' stream, a relatively backward child is able to work alongside others of comparable ability, is protected therefore from invidious comparisons with those who are better endowed and the consequent discouragement that must inevitably follow from finding himself outwitted and outpaced by them. (It may be interpolated that in arguments put forward in defence of streaming, 'B'-stream children are rarely instanced. Is this, one wonders, because they are neither afforded stimulation, nor protected from discouragement?)

Streaming has always attracted criticism, but since the 1950s this has steadily increased in volume and intensity and has been accompanied by positive action: there is now a non-streaming 'movement' and a substantial number of schools—mainly primary but some secondary as well—have 'unstreamed' to varying extents. Some have done this partially—streaming some year-groups but not others, for example, or retaining a 'C' stream, but blurring the distinction between the 'A's' and 'B's'; others have gone the whole hog, introducing what the Americans describe as 'planned heterogeneity'. The progress of this non-streaming movement has been documented in the pages of the journal *Forum* and some of these articles have been collected together and published by Professor Brian Simon (Simon, 1964).

The criticisms that are levelled against streaming have a familiar ring, in that they echo those that are frequently used to oppose the practice of selection. The first is that the declared objectives of streaming cannot possibly be attained. Its purpose is to yield homogeneous groups. A pertinent question in this regard is: homogeneous with respect to what? If, for example, we wish to assemble, in a primary school, a class that exhibits a narrow range of attainments in English—a group that comprises children whose levels of reading comprehension, for instance, are broadly comparable—we shall find, when we turn to some other subject, such as mathematics, that we are confronted with a set of pupils whose capacities and interests are much more varied. Add to this the facts that we examined earlier concerning the unreliability of any forms of assessment that we may choose for this purpose, and it must be recognized that streaming is a coarse, unsatisfactory and potentially unjust form of grouping.

The remaining objections are concerned with the supposed effects of streaming and bring us, therefore, into disputed territory. It is maintained, by those who oppose streaming, that, no matter how streamed classes may be designated, the children concerned readily perceive the significance of the procedure. Those assigned to the lower streams develop a sense of inferiority which reduces their motivation and hinders their progress; those in the top streams may suffer anxiety as a result of the pressures that compel them to justify their status or may develop inflated notions concerning their intellectual superiority. As children advance through a streamed school the gulf that was alleged to separate them at the outset perceptibly widens, partly as a result of the discouragement suffered by children in the lower streams, and partly because of the tendency, notable in many schools, to assign the most effective teachers to the abler children. The critics of streaming, unlike its supporters, do mention the children in 'B' classes, alleging that here particularly there is a marked wastage of talent. A final objection is that, no matter how allocation to separate streams is determined, children from the less favourable home backgrounds tend to find themselves in the lower streams: this, it has been suggested, is tantamount to imposing an extra handicap on someone who has already had a bad start.

Research into streaming

These direct conflicts of view on the operation and effects of streaming have prompted a large number of investigations, most of which, unfortunately, have been too poorly designed to yield interpretable results. The studies are so numerous as to call for a sizeable number of separate reviews of their findings. In the suggestions for further reading reference will be made to these reviews as well as to the major studies that merit special attention. Of these there are two (Goldberg *et al.*, 1966 and Barker-Lunn, 1970) which, taken together, provide enough well-attested evidence to provide a basis for judging the issues we have been considering.

The Goldberg study was of an experimental kind: forty-five New York elementary schools took part and the children concerned were re-grouped to provide classes of varying ranges of ability—some very narrow (equivalent to 'A' and 'C' streams in junior schools in this country) and some accommodating the full available range (equivalent to non-streamed classes). The Barker-Lunn investigation, conducted by the National Foundation for Educational Research, was, on the other hand, 'operational': it involved detailed comparisons between pupils in thirty-six streamed schools with those in thirty-six non-streamed schools.

The reader is advised to study the results of both these investigations in detail. We must content ourselves here with a bare summary of the major findings.

The crucial issue is the extent to which streaming or non-streaming is found to exert the more favourable influence on children's academic progress and attainments. The Goldberg study found little difference between the levels of attainment of pupils in 'narrow-range' or 'broad-range' classes: such differences as could be detected were not educationally significant and were in favour of the

83

broad-range or non-streamed classes. The Barker-Lunn inquiry revealed no difference between streamed and non-streamed schools in the average academic performances of pupils of comparable ability and social class. In the American investigation there was no apparent difference either with respect to a whole range of non-academic variables: measures of, for example, children's interests, social development and their attitudes towards schooling. The Foundation's inquiry, however, revealed some differences in this respect: although children of above-average ability fared equally well in each type of school, there was evidence that those of average and below-average ability in non-streamed schools developed more favourable attitudes to schoolwork and better relations with their teachers than did their counterparts in streamed schools.

Although none of the studies previous to these two large-scale and well-controlled investigations could be relied upon to yield generalizable results, taken together they may be considered to add considerable weight to the evidence we have just examined. Overall, they serve to confirm the conclusions we have outlined: that, if we adopt as our sole criterion the academic achievements of the pupils concerned, there is nothing to choose between a streamed or a non-streamed form of organization; if, however, we consider a wider range of effects—such as the children's motivation, interest in school work, and relations with their teachers—non-streaming would seem to offer distinct advantages.

Setting

An alternative to streaming that is commonly found in secondary schools, although rarely at the primary level, is described as 'setting', and involves grouping pupils for certain subjects or activities with reference to their relevant levels of attainment or rate of progress. Thus one might have non-streamed classes which, for a limited number of periods—those devoted to mathematics or foreign languages, for example—are reorganized into relatively homogeneous groups. The Goldberg study, to which we have just referred, although finding no evidence in support of streaming, reports results which suggest that setting, even in the primary school, may have a favourable effect on children's attainments. The researches—although limited in number—that have so far been carried out into the outcome of setting in secondary schools, have also provided favourable indications (Yates, 1966).

Grouping within classes

To round off the account we should note that grouping is not necessarily at an end when pupils have been assigned to classes of whatever kind. Dividing a class into further sub-groups is a common practice. Even at this level we find divergences of view amongst teachers concerning the ways in which this operation can be most effectively conducted. Some carry out a miniature form of streaming, segregating the pupils on the basis of their abilities or average attainments; others prefer to form mixed-ability groups. In some classes, the groups, however composed, are kept together; in others there is considerable fluidity, with fresh combinations of pupils for each subject or activity. Some teachers wholly determine the assignment of pupils to groups; others permit a degree of choice to the children themselves. Although there is some evidence to suggest that intra-class grouping yields somewhat higher levels of achievement than whole-class teaching (Ebel, 1969), little research has as yet been undertaken into the relative merits of the different patterns that it can assume.

4

Conclusions and reflections

Most of the readers of this book will eventually become parents—if they have not already achieved this distinction; many are presumably intending to teach; some may one day occupy influential positions in politics or administration. Few, if any, therefore, can expect to avoid becoming directly involved in the issues that we have been considering. The conclusions and reflections with which this final section is concerned should, accordingly, be the reader's own. To this end, it is proposed to offer a number of suggestions and questions for discussion rather than to attempt to provide neat solutions and firm recommendations. In spite of this disclaimer the reader should be warned, perhaps, against the risk of allowing himself to be unduly influenced by the author's predilections which he has not strenuously attempted to conceal.

When, at the outset, we were looking ahead to this review of grouping practices it was suggested that one characteristic that they have in common is that they all attract criticism in some measure. Now that we are able to look back on our survey, we might be tempted to conclude that another characteristic that they broadly share is that of irrelevance. This is too strong a term, of course. But there is a good deal of evidence to be found—some of which we have already examined—to support the view that many of the forms of grouping that we have seen fit to introduce, often at a considerable cost in terms of administrative effort, have at best only a marginal effect on the educational progress of the pupils for whom they have been designed. Large-scale surveys, such as those conducted by the International Project for the Evaluation of Educational Achievement (Husen, 1967), in which attempts are made to attribute portions of the variance in children's attainments to the various factors that may be supposed to influence it, have shown that only a relatively small fraction is accounted for by aspects of school organization. Among the variables over which we can exercise some control in designing educational arrangements, it will come perhaps as no surprise to learn that it is the transactions that take place between teachers and pupils—in whatever organizational setting they might find themselves—that exert the major influences on the eventual outcome.

In the light of these indications, we might usefully reflect on some of the major forms of grouping that have occupied our attention and question the extent to which their use would seem to be warranted.

Chronological age

We saw that there was broad agreement that a child's age is an important factor to take into account both in assigning pupils to different kinds of school and in ordering educational arrangements within schools. We saw too that this agreement gives way to a considerable amount of uncertainty when we come to face the practical decisions concerning the precise ages to be chosen as the boundaries between the groups that are to be formed. What is interesting and perhaps significant to note is that all the various patterns proposed appear at least to be viable. Children of primary age may be housed within one establishment from the ages of five to eleven; or they may be allocated to separate infants' and junior schools. For children between the ages of eleven and eighteen a variety of patterns have been adopted with apparent success. Sixth-form colleges have earned the approval of those who have taught and studied in them—disaster does not appear to overtake a secondary school that forfeits its senior pupils to this kind of establishment. On the other hand some 'all-through' schools are manifestly going concerns, and there is ample evidence to show that middle schools housing the nine to thirteen range can be successfully promoted.

When we come to examine the misgivings that are expressed concerning one or other of these patterns we are afforded an insight which serves to explain some of the difficulties that beset this and other forms of grouping. It will be recalled that objections to the use of chronological age to determine the point of transfer from one school or department to another centred round the fact that children manifest a wide range of individual differences with respect to their progress and development. At any given age, therefore, they exhibit different degrees of readiness for whatever the next phase of their formal education has to offer. One specific example to which we referred concerned those children who enter secondary schools whilst still unable to read adequately, and are often not provided there with the skilled attention that they require. We need not interpret this difficulty, however, as one that stems from a decision to group children in this fashion but rather as a manifest failure to make adequate provision within the schools concerned to meet the needs of some of their pupils. It may be regarded as perfectly sensible, on a number of grounds, to choose the age of eleven as the point of transfer from primary to secondary schools. The problems that this and other comparable decisions have created are the result of attaching undue educational significance to what can deservedly be regarded only as a matter of administrative convenience. We may be said to have re-discovered, in this context, an obvious truth: that a school can operate successfully only if it adapts its arrangements to suit the ascertained needs of its pupils rather than expecting the pupils to accommodate themselves to its preconceptions.

These considerations do not justify the conclusion that grouping with reference to chronological age may be regarded as unnecessary but they serve perhaps to take the sharp edge from the controversies that surround the topic. We are not absolved from the need to investigate the possibility that one pattern may be more convenient and effective than another, but in the meantime we can take comfort from the fact that by a suitable redeployment of staff and by choosing an appropriate form of internal organization we can offer adequate educational provision for any chosen age-range.

Grouping by ability

When one considers the difficulties involved in devising and operating a procedure designed to choose candidates for grammar or other kinds of selective school, it becomes apparent that the undertaking could be justified only if its benefits were demonstrably significant. In the event, we have seen that no advantages can be claimed on its behalf. There is no available evidence to suggest that those children who, at eleven, are judged to be among the ablest of their year-group suffer any handicap if they are housed within a comprehensive school. On the other hand those who appear to be somewhat less able are found to make much more favourable progress in these circumstances.

Although we have ample empirical justification for doubting the effectiveness of segregating pupils in terms of their measured 'intelligence', we could have predicted the outcome on theoretical grounds. The fact that among the instruments readily available for the purposes of selection, intelligence tests were demonstrably the most highly predictive, has led to an exaggerated estimate of the role that the attributes measured in this way play in determining scholastic success. The results of a number of surveys have demonstrated that measured intelligence accounts for as little as 16 to 25 per cent of the variation in academic attainments. Three-quarters of the determination of achievement must thus be attributed to other factors. Intelligence tests enable us to distinguish fairly satisfactorily between groups of children: average scores are quite reliable indices of the characteristics of the group as a whole. They do not permit us, however, to make accurate predictions on behalf of an individual. Given two children of the same intelligence we may expect that they will achieve at the same level; that one may be a spectacular success and the other an abysmal failure; or any other possibility in between.

If this is the case—and there is a wealth of evidence to support it—why, one might ask, has selection worked at all. (We have seen that it does not work very well, but rather better perhaps than this evidence would lead us to suppose.) The answer would seem to lie in the fact that children tend to be obliging. If we give them a good or bad name, they prefer to live up to it rather than to embarrass us by falsifying our predictions. This 'self-fulfilling prophecy' is not an invention conjured up by those who object to the selective system. There is a good deal of evidence to show that the levels of expectation that teachers set with regard to their pupils' performance exert a marked influence on the standards that are in fact achieved (Pidgeon, 1970).

Allocating children to separate schools on the basis of their measured ability also has unfortunate social consequences. A child who is assigned to one of two or three distinct kinds of school that enjoy different degrees of prestige will inevitably conclude that the society to which he belongs comprises a corresponding number of groups of citizens—the other sort and us. And the accompanying sense of superiority and inferiority—for which, as we have seen, there is inadequate justification—can only be heightened when it comes to be recognized that the schools concerned differ not only in repute as educational establishments but also substantially determine their pupils' future vocational status and material prosperity. If our aspirations to become one nation have any genuine basis we surely cannot tolerate this form of institutionalized privilege.

The case for abandoning this form of grouping is often regarded, even when the force of the argument is admitted, as being of a somewhat negative kind. It is perceived as an attempt simply to put a stop to arrangements that tend to offer advantages to only one section of the community. It may be represented, however, as a means not only of satisfying a proper demand for equality of opportunity but also as one of increasing in a real and positive sense the range of opportunities open to every pupil. A comprehensive school may be expected to contribute to the cohesiveness of society but not to obscure individual differences. Indeed it is arguable that the potentially rich variety of its composition will encourage the development of a wide range of talents. Academic excellence is only one form of accomplishment. When it can be encouraged to flourish alongside others, both those who achieve it and those who do not may be enabled to set it in adequate perspective. A school of all the talents furnishes an opportunity not simply for an élite to emerge but for a series of élites, and for them to do so in circumstances which make it possible for their members to escape the sense of isolation that their early segregation engenders. If we were to commit ourselves wholeheartedly to the comprehensive concept and set about discovering, by processes of research and development, the most suitable form of organization for schools of this kind we might well be able—to paraphrase Lionel Elvin—to create a country fit for élites to live in.

Grouping by social class

This form of grouping which involves the co-existence of a private and a public sector need scarcely detain us. On social grounds, the choice is clear, depending on one's taste for, and one's capacity to justify, the kind of society that this kind of arrangement reflects and serves to sustain. On educational grounds, there would be seen to be no evidence to suggest that independence *per se* can be held responsible for the high standards that some of these schools maintain. It is much more likely that the contributing factors are the facilities and amenities that many of these schools are able to provide; the services of a dedicated staff; and possibly the extra tuition and supervision that boarding makes possible. All these are features that can be represented in maintained schools—and, of course, in some of them they manifestly are. Even if independence could be shown to have some bearing on the outcome, a degree of this, too, could conceivably be introduced into the publicly provided system. Some devolution of responsibility for the ordering of a school's affairs might be passed to the governing body on which both teachers and parents were substantially represented. Moves in this direction have already been made by some local education authorities. On the other hand, there are no grounds for believing that, in the present circumstances, the Heads and staffs of maintained schools find themselves any less free to exercise their professional responsibilities than their counterparts in independent schools.

92

Grouping by sex

Our review of the evidence concerning the differences between the educational needs manifested by boys and girls revealed that these were not sufficiently large to justify separate treatment—at least to the extent of housing them in single-sex schools. We found, moreover, that the differences within the sexes in this regard are considerably greater than those between them. Since we saw also that there is considerable empirical evidence to support the view that children's levels of achievement tend to be higher in co-educational than in single-sex schools, we might conclude that there is no apparent need to resort to this form of grouping. Indeed a convincing case can be put forward that in terms of the degree of mutual understanding that it fosters and the resultant attitudes that boys and girls develop towards each other, co-education has considerable benefits to confer.

Grouping by religious denomination

Although some of those concerned would not yet be prepared to fall in with the suggestion, it is arguable that this form of grouping, too, could be advantageously dispensed with. Any form of segregation serves to emphasize the distinctions on which it is based, and one would suppose that it would be in the general interest to lay stress on shared attributes and purposes rather than to advertise, as it were, differences in religious faith and practice. Making appropriate provision within a common school for distinctive forms of religious instruction would not be unduly difficult.

Grouping within schools

Of those forms of grouping within schools that are intended to form broad divisions for administrative and social purposes, nothing may be said, since there is no available evidence concerning their relative effectiveness. We may justifiably question the necessity of streaming, however, on much the same grounds as those on which selection for different kinds of school has been opposed. Even the most generous interpretation of the evidence that has been accumulated on this issue, would be that streaming is no more effective a form of organization than those much simpler alternatives which obviate the need for assessing the abilities and aptitudes of all entrants. And one may suppose that, if it were rigidly operated, its socially divisive effects could be almost as pronounced as those that may be attributed to selection.

We know much less about the practice of setting, and such evidence as we have suggests that this might well be a serviceable device. It is of course, in principle, markedly different from streaming. The latter involves a total judgment which carries with it, for those consigned to the lower streams, the kind of stigma that is attached to the secondary-modern school within the tripartite system. In a school, however, within which such judgments were, as a matter of policy, avoided and within which, for many of their activities, the pupils were grouped in a recognizably heterogeneous form, a certain amount of setting could well serve the school's avowed purpose of attempting to develop each child's talents to the full. There would seem to be nothing immoral or in any other sense untoward in bringing together like-minded people for some pursuits. That some of the students who showed a marked aptitude for, and unusual degree of interest in, mathematics should associate for lessons in this subject, is just as defensible

94

as electing the best eleven footballers to play in the school team. Such a practice, one would have thought, can harm neither those who belong to, nor those who are excluded from, a particular set. It is when such arrangements are a permanent feature of a school's organization that one might find the self-fulfilling prophecy exerting its baleful influence. We surmised that a system of separate schools, differing in prestige, would lead the pupils to suppose that there are three kinds of citizen, each allotted to his specific role and status in society. We conjectured, too, that a streamed organization might be interpreted by the pupils concerned in a similar way. How, one might ask, are they likely to regard the kind of organization that we have just described: one, that is, that is mainly characterized by heterogeneous groups but which, for some purposes, reconstitutes these into sets composed of individuals with similar levels of attainment? A reasonable expectation might be that the pupils would learn to regard their society as one which offered common rights and shared responsibilities but in which certain forms of accomplishment—scientific, artistic, athletic, etc.—could be distinguished and rewarded in their own right and in which opportunities for individual advancement and growth in the various aspects of living are not contingent upon each other.

Setting, of course, is not the only form of grouping that might achieve this objective. Certain kinds of team teaching and other flexible grouping arrangements might be equally advantageous. There are some teachers, too, who believe that with appropriate kinds of intra-class grouping and an organization that makes provision for individualized instruction, homogeneous grouping can profitably be dispensed with altogether. There is obviously considerable scope within the area of school organization for research into the effectiveness of different grouping patterns.

Concluding note

We have referred in this final section to all but two of the bases of grouping that were considered earlier: grouping in accordance with a child's place of residence, and that which takes into account his special needs or disabilities. The former may be briefly dismissed since, for most children, it must inevitably serve as a factor in determining the school he attends. The problem that it involves, as we have noted, is that in some instances neighbourhood schools may prove to be unwontedly homogeneous.

We may usefully end our survey with a reference to special schools, not because there is anything controversial about the grouping that they involve, but rather on the grounds that declared public policy in this respect embodies a principle which, in the light of the foregoing discussion, we might feel could be more broadly extended. The Department of Education and Science requires local education authorities to place certain categories of pupils in special schools. In defining these categories, however, it is emphasized that 'it is the national policy that handicapped children shall be educated in ordinary schools unless their disability renders this impracticable or undesirable' (Education Act 1944, Section 33).

The evidence that we have reviewed might be thought to support the hypothesis that this would serve as a viable policy with regard to all children. If the common, neighbourhood school became the norm there is no reason to suppose, in the light of our present knowledge, that any child's welfare or prospects need be adversely affected, and ample grounds for expecting that society generally would reap benefits from the arrangement. It could conceivably enable the children of this country to attain parity of esteem.

Bibliography

Advisory Council for Education, *Early Leaving*, H.M.S.O., 1954.

BAIR, M. and WOODWARD, R. G., *Team Teaching in Action*, Houghton, 1964.

BARKER-LUNN, J. C., *Streaming in the Primary School*, N.F.E.R., 1970.

DALE, R. R., 'Co-education I', *Educational Research*, Vol. 4, No. 3, 1962.

—— 'Co-education II', *Educational Research*, Vol. 5, No. 1, 1962.

—— 'Co-education III', *Educational Research*, Vol. 6, No. 3, 1964.

—— *Mixed or Single-sex School?*, Vol. I, Routledge & Kegan Paul, 1969.

DANCY, J. C., *The Public Schools and the Future*, Faber, 1963.

EBEL, R. L. (ed.), *Encyclopaedia of Educational Research* (article on 'Grouping' by Heathers, G.), Macmillan, 1969.

ERIKSON, E. H., *Childhood and society*, Norton, 1963.

FLAVELL, J. H., *The Development Psychology of Jean Piaget*, Van Nostrand, 1963.

GOLDBERG, M. L., PASSOW, A. H. and JUSTMAN, J., *The Effects of Ability Grouping*, Columbia: Teachers College, 1966.

HEBB, D. O., *The Organisation of Behavior*, John Wiley, 1949.

HUNT, J. MCV., *Intelligence and Experience*, Ronald Press, 1961.

HUSEN, T. (ed.), *International Study of Achievement in Mathematics*, John Wiley, 1967.

—— and SVENSON, N. E., 'Pedagogic milieu and the development of intellectual skills', *School Review*, 1960.

LAMBERT, ROYSTON, *The Hothouse Society*, Weidenfeld & Nicolson, 1968.

MICHELSON, J., 'What does research say about the effectiveness of the core curriculum?', *School Review*, 1967.

MONKS, T. G., *Comprehensive Education in England and Wales*, N.F.E.R., 1968.

MORRIS, J. M., *Standards and Progress in Reading*, N.F.E.R., 1966.

PEDLEY, R., *The Comprehensive School*, Pelican, 1963.

PIAGET, J., *The Origins of Intelligence in Children*, Routledge & Kegan Paul, 1952.

PIDGEON, D. A., *Expectation and Pupil Performance*, Stockholm: Almquist and Wiksell, 1970.

—— and YATES, A., *An Introduction to Educational Measurement*, Routledge & Kegan Paul, 1968.

Public Schools Commission, *First Report*, H.M.S.O., 1968.

—— *Second Report*, H.M.S.O., 1970.

SEARS, R. R., 'Identification as a form of behaviour development', in Harris D. B. (ed.), *The Concept of Development*, Univ. of Minnesota, 1967.

SHAPLIN, J. T. and OLDS, H. F., *Team Teaching*, Harper and Row, 1964.

SIGEL, I. E. and HOOPER, F. H., *Logical Thinking in Children*, Holt, Rinehart, and Winston, 1968.

SIMON, B. (ed.), *Non-streaming in the Junior School*, Leicester: PSW (Educational) Publications, 1964.

SVENSON, N. E., *Ability Grouping and Scholastic Achievement*, Uppsala: Almquist and Wiksell, 1962.

TERMAN, L. M. and TYLER, L. E., 'Psychological sex differences', in Carmichael, L. (ed.), *Manual of Child Psychology*, John Wiley, 1954.

VERNON, P. E., *The Structure of Human Abilities*, Methuen, 1961.

YATES, A. (ed.), *Grouping in Education*, John Wiley, 1966.

Suggestions for further reading

1 *General*

Yates, A. (ed.), *Grouping in Education*, John Wiley, 1966.
This reports the findings of a group of educationists, drawn
from eight different countries, who collated and reviewed
the available research evidence on grouping practices. It
also contains nearly fifty abstracts of relevant research
reports.

Thelen, H. A., *Classroom Grouping for Teachability*, John
Wiley, 1967.
Although dealing in the main with one specific aspect of
grouping, this book contains, in its introductory chapters,
a useful review of, and insightful comments on, a wide
range of problems in this field.

Elvin, H. L., *Education and Contemporary Society*, Watts,
1965.
A perceptive analysis of the relationship between various
patterns of school organization and the needs of contemporary society.

2 *Assigning pupils to schools*
   (a) *General*
   Dent, H. C., *The Educational System of England and
   Wales*, University of London Press, 1969.
   A detailed description of the present system and the
   kinds of school that it comprises.

(b) *Single-sex v. co-educational schools*
Dale, R. R., *Mixed or Single-sex School?*, Routledge & Kegan Paul, 1969.
This is the first of four books, designed to report the author's twenty years of study in this field. The total series should help to settle this issue.

(c) *Independent schools*
Public Schools Commission, *First and Second Reports*, H.M.S.O., 1968, 1970.
The Newson and Donnison reports: facts and figures that cannot be disputed; recommendations that are.

Dancy, J. C., *The Public Schools and the Future*, Faber, 1963, and Wilson, John, *Public Schools and Private Practice*, Allen and Unwin, 1962.
These two books state the case for the public schools and for spreading their benefits more widely.

Howarth, T. E. B., *Culture, Anarchy and the Public Schools*, Cassell, 1969.
A defence of the situation as it is, or perhaps a hankering after what it used to be. It contains so much that is patronizing and obscurantist that only those already well disposed towards the public schools are likely to be able to stomach it.

Lambert, Royston, *The Hothouse Society*, Weidenfeld & Nicolson, 1968.
In which the pupils are allowed to speak for themselves.

Lambert, Royston, *et al.*, *New Wine in Old Bottles*, Bell, 1968.
Contains some empirical studies of what happens within

public schools when their entry is broadened. Highly relevant to the discussion of 'integration'.

N.U.T., *Memorandum of Evidence Submitted to the Commission on Public Schools.*
A manual for forthright abolitionists.

(d) *Selective* v. *comprehensive schools*
Yates, A. and Pidgeon, D. A., *Admission to Grammar Schools*, Newnes, 1957 and Vernon, P. E. (ed.), *Secondary School Selection*, Methuen, 1957.
These books review the problems associated with selection for secondary education and the results of a considerable volume of relevant research.

Rubinstein, David and Simon, Brian, *The Evolution of the Comprehensive School*, Routledge & Kegan Paul, 1969 and Pedley, R., *The Comprehensive School*, Pelican, 1963.
These provide an account of the development of comprehensive education in this country and a record of its achievements.

Rée, H. A., *The Essential Grammar School*, Harrap, 1956 and Davies, H., *Culture and the Grammar School*, University of Nottingham Institute of Education, 1965.
A discussion of the distinctive contribution that grammar schools have to make and a plea for their continued existence.

Svenson, N. E., *Ability Grouping and Scholastic Achievement*, Uppsala : Almquist and Wiksell, 1962 and Husen, T. and Svenson, N. E., 'Pedagogic milieu and development of intellectual skills', *School Review*, 1960.

An account of Swedish researches designed to compare selective and comprehensive schools.

Husen, T. (ed.), *International Study of Achievement in Mathematics* (2 vols.), John Wiley, 1967.
Contains a wealth of research evidence relating to the effects of different patterns of grouping.

3   *Grouping within schools*
    (a)   *Patterns of school organization*
    Monks, T. G., *Comprehensive Education in England and Wales*, N.F.E.R., 1968.

    (b)   *Team teaching*
    Shaplin, J. T. and Olds, H. F., *Team Teaching*, Harper and Row, 1964.
    An account of the origin and rationale of team teaching, with accounts of investigations designed to test its effectiveness.

    (c)   *Streaming and setting*
    Yates, A. (*op. cit.*).
    This contains references to, and some abstracts of, relevant research carried out in a number of countries.

    Goldberg, M. L., Passow, A. H. and Justman, J., *The Effects of Ability Grouping*, Columbia: Teachers College, 1966.
    The best-designed experimental study yet carried out in this field.

    Barker-Lunn, J. C., *Streaming in the Primary School*, N.F.E.R., 1970.
    A comprehensive and detailed operational study of streaming in this country.